GOOD MORNING, EVERYBODY!
An assembly book for 4–9-year-olds.

GOOD MORNING, EVERYBODY!
EVERYBODY!
An assembly book for 4 – 9-year-olds

Redvers Brandling

Basil Blackwell

© 1986 Redvers Brandling
First published 1986

Published by
Basil Blackwell Limited
108 Cowley Road
Oxford OX4 1JF
England

British Library Cataloguing in Publication Data

Brandling, Redvers
   Good morning, everybody! an assembly book for 4 - 9 year olds.
   1. Schools—Exercises and recreations—Great Britain   2. School—
   Great Britain—Prayers
   I. Title
   377'.1   LB3015

ISBN   0-631-15074-9

Typeset in 10 on 12pt Times Roman
by Multiplex Techniques Ltd, St Mary Cray, Kent.
Printed in Great Britain

Contents

Acknowledgements

I am, as always, grateful to the staff and children of Dewhurst St Mary School, Cheshunt, from whom I have learnt so much by watching and listening to many assembly presentations.

Many books are mentioned in the text and in Appendix 2. I am indebted to them for both inspiration and information. It should also be mentioned that some of the stories in this book have been used, heard, and re-adapted several times in assemblies. In consequence their original sources are not remembered and if this has unwittingly caused the infringement of copyright, the author apologises and will correct this omission in future editions, if notified.

The author and publisher would like to thank the following for permission to reproduce copyright material:

The Royal Life Saving Society for the extract from the 'Blue Code' (p 24); Simon and Schuster Inc for 'Can't Wait' by John Kitching (p 32) and 'When I learned to whistle' by Gordon Lea (p 108) both from *Miracles* by Richard Lewis; William Collins, Sons & Co Ltd for a prayer (p 68) from *Prayers for Young People* by William Barclay; David Higham Ltd for 'Lady' (p 96) from *Your Obedient Servant* by Angela Patmore, published by Hutchinson; Andre Deutsch Ltd for 'Mum's coming home today' (p 116) from *Mind your own business* by Michael Rosen; the estate of Elizabeth Stucley for 'Spring' (p 128) from *Magnolia Buildings* by Elizabeth Stucley, published by The Bodley Head; Galliard Ltd for 'Sowing Seed' (p 137) by Anthony Geering; Christian Education Movement for the prayer by Kim Chi Ha (p 149) from *Food;* Stainer and Bell Ltd for 'Mary set out on a winter's night' by Susan Moxom.

'Raksha Bandhan' (p 24) is adapted from a piece of the same name which appeared in *First Focus* by Redvers Brandling (Bell & Hyman, 1984). 'Gifts' by Olive Kershaw (p 85) is reproduced by kind permission of High-Fye Music Ltd, 78 Newman St, London W1P 3LA (Used by permission. All rights reserved.)

Every effort has been made to trace the source of copyright material and it is regretted if any acknowledgement has been unwittingly omitted.

Introduction

'Religious Education starts with where people are, and as they are.' (*Hello World*, G Bennett and I Tiernan)

It would be difficult to quibble with this statement, yet if it is applied to infant and first schools it immediately focuses attention upon many of the difficulties which face those who take assemblies with young children.

To begin with, young children have very limited experience. What little they do have is gained from first-hand contact with families and communities, from relationships and communication with each other and with adults. This, however, is an advantage in that they have already come into contact with 'thematic' issues such as concern, sharing, joy, compassion, forgiveness etc in a practical sense.

The tasks of the assembly presenter in infant and first schools include fostering exploration, development and extension of this practical experience; increasing children's awareness; and providing opportunities for increased sharing and extended experiences.

This book is designed to help in meeting these aims. It does so through three main sections:

Section 1 provides direct assembly material. It contains over 60 complete assemblies, each of which has a short passage to 'set the scene'; a story; thoughts/prayers; a hymn suggestion; and notes on further talking points, additional information and references. Each of these assemblies could be used 'instantly', with little or no preparation – although this would obviously increase their potential. The stories chosen come from a wide variety of sources: folk tales, religious books, newscuttings, magazines, poems and factual accounts.

With young children a wide range of themes can sometimes lead to confusion, so the assemblies in Section 1 are divided into four main themes:

People: to admire, to think about, to wonder at, to relate to . . .
Creatures: seen here in a real life context, as well as a symbolic one – and of great interest to young children.
Qualities: a very far-ranging theme which will incorporate a wide variety of qualities to which the teacher might want to draw attention.
Special occasions: here stories may follow on from an occasion, or alternatively lead back to further consideration of the event.

Of course, within this subdivision of themes there are many other interwoven topics, which teachers can draw out as and when they choose.

Section 2 offers 10 detailed assemblies which involve children in class assembly presentations. Class assemblies do not exist in a vacuum. They are the product of a considerable amount of work in the classroom. They often include many curriculum areas – particularly reading, drama, art, creative writing and environmental studies. With this body of knowledge and preparation built into them, they provide a marvellous opportunity to 'celebrate together'. They also give the added bonus of providing more talking points, thoughts and follow-up ideas, which can be taken back to other classrooms, and which are often the seeds for future presentations.

At the school where I work we always invite the parents of children taking an assembly to be with us for the presentation. The parents are involved in the hymns and prayers and sometimes contribute in other ways, such as choral speaking. Their presence helps to make the assembly a genuine community occasion, and afterwards they stay behind for a short while to look in more detail at the preparation work the children have done.

A word of warning seems necessary – class assemblies should not be too frequent. As a rough guide, one class assembly per class per term is recommended. This allows plenty of time for preparation and also gives the children the sense of being involved in something special.

The section on class assemblies provides initial background information on the purpose/aim of each assembly, and describes materials needed, necessary preparation and numbers involved. Each assembly lasts about 15 minutes.

Section 3 concentrates on the use of drama in assembly. Somtimes this can be introduced *ad lib* – as when the presenter says 'I need somebody to help me' and uses a child or children as 'props' in telling a story. Mainly, however, drama in assembly falls into three categories, which each offer opportunities for a wide-ranging involvement.

1 Drama where there is *action*, linked with reading from scripts.
2 Drama where there is *miming* to a commentary or commentaries.
3 Drama where the action has been scripted, cast, learnt, rehearsed – and is presented in *play* form.

Section 3 provides a lengthy list of subjects with potential for development as assembly material. These are 'starters' which the class teacher can build on in her own way. Two or three of these starters are then looked at in more detail, with suggestions about how they could be built up in an improvised way. Finally, there are examples to two written-up plays, based on the initial dramatic ideas.

The aim of this book is essentially practical. It seeks to provide a range of material which can be used 'instantly'; which can be developed along individual lines; and which can be as wide-ranging as the teacher chooses to make it. The materials have been chosen to be as fresh as possible, and also to fulfil the needs of a multi-cultural environment. Finally, we have tried to make the presentation as clear as possible, so that the busy teacher is not faced with complicated cross-referencing in the search for lively and thought-provoking assemblies.

Section 1
Complete Assemblies

Introduction

The assemblies which follow can be used at short notice. Each has the essential elements to hand – some introductory comments to set the scene; a story; a prayer; a hymn suggestion.

In a sense, however, these elements are merely the ingredients for the meal. It is the 'recipe' for preparation and presentation which results in the quality of the end product. It is my firm belief that, with infants in particular, a story well told is better than a story well read. One of my reasons for this preference is the skill which I have seen so many infant teachers use in establishing a marvellous rapport between storyteller and listeners. The stories in this section are therefore written in a way which alows them to be readily assimilated for re-telling.

It might also be mentioned here that all the stories have been used with children in the first school age group. It was found advantageous with many of them to use 'instant' props – children and materials immediately to hand. For instance in *A cat has nine lives* (page 80) a much greater sense of involvement is achieved if children picked at random from the audience represent Hans, the kitten and the lady as the story unfolds. Similarly the story of the helicopter rescue was enhanced by the lowering of one of the climbing ropes in the hall to give some idea of how difficult it would be to catch a swinging rope while in a heaving lifeboat.

Resourceful infant assembly presenters will no doubt have their own ideas about how these stories can be best projected. In keeping with this idea the provision of a little extra background material to 'flesh out' the subject has been included in most of the individual packages.

The garden

Introduction

This morning's story is about a family who had to move from their house to live in a flat. Jimmy and his mummy and daddy weren't sure how they would like the flat – particularly daddy, who had loved his garden.

Story

It all started when Jimmy saw Mum reading the magazine. It was different from what she usually read. It was full of pictures of spades and tools and lawn mowers.

'What are you reading, Mum?' asked Jimmy.

Mum smiled and pushed a stray piece of hair out of her eyes. Jimmy thought she looked sad for some reason.

'Just a magazine,' she answered. 'You see it's daddy's birthday the day after next and I'm looking to see if I can find anything he would like.'

'Oh', said Jimmy. He looked over Mum's shoulder at the magazine and then he looked at her again. Now he knew why she was sad. It was all those pictures of lawn mowers. Since the family had moved into this block of flats Jimmy had often heard Dad say how much he missed their old garden.

'Look', he would say, picking Jimmy up and putting him on his shoulders. 'Nowhere to plant even a cabbage down there.'

And Jimmy would look through the window and down to where all the cars and buses moved about like Dinky toys.

'Jimmy,' Mum's voice interrupted his thoughts. 'It's tea time. Come on. I've got some of your favourite cream buns.'

The magazine about lawn mowers was under the TV set and mum had her cheerful face on now.

'Smashing,' said Jimmy. But all the same he hadn't forgotten about Dad's birthday and that garden.

It was after he and Mum had been out shopping the next morning that Jimmy had the idea. When they moved to the flat, Dad had used two wooden boxes to carry things in. Afterwards he had taken them to pieces and put them in the storeroom downstairs.

'Mum, can I get some of Dad's wood?'

'All right dear,' said Mum, 'but what do you want it for?'

'Just to make something.'

Mum unlocked the storeroom. The door was bright blue and it had silver numbers saying 27 on it'.

'What a mess,' sighed Mum as they looked at the pile of suitcases, Jimmy's old pushchair and the sledge. But Jimmy could see what he wanted.

When they got back upstairs Jimmy took the pieces of wood into his bedroom. Then he got some newspapers from Mum and spread them on the floor. Next he got the tools Dad had given him for Christmas. Soon he was very busy with his hammer and nails.

That night Mum rang up Gran as she did every Wednesday. She always let Jimmy speak to Gran too.

'Is that you Jimmy?' said Gran, the way she always did.

'Yes,' said Jimmy. 'Will you get me something, Gran?'

'Oh, what's that then?' asked Gran.

Jimmy quickly told Gran what he wanted. He did it quickly because Mum had gone into the kitchen to switch the kettle off and he didn't want her to hear.

The next day was Dad's birthday. Mum made a special tea and she said Dad was going to get all his presents then. Gran arrived at dinner time.

'Whatever have you got there?' asked Mum as she let Gran in.

'Never you mind,' said Gran in between puffs and gasps. She carried the heavy looking shopping bag to Jimmy's bedroom. Opening the door in front of her, he followed her inside.

When teatime came Dad was back. He had a special cake, and he and Mum and Gran all laughed at the candles which spelled out 'Dad'. He got a pair of slippers from Gran and a new pipe from Mum. Jimmy didn't say anything until Dad had finished looking at these presents.

'Dad.'

'Yes Jimmy?'

'I've got something for you.'

'Have you? That's lovely, Jimmy.'

'It's in my bedroom.'

'Come on then, what are we waiting for?'

Whizzing Jimmy round in his arms, Dad went into the bedroom. Gran followed, smiling, and so did Mum – looking very puzzled.

'There!' said Jimmy, flinging open the door.

'Why,' said Dad, 'it's just what I wanted. It's a . . . it's a garden!'

Jimmy looked at the box he'd made. It was filled with soil Gran had brought. Then he saw the white packet she had brought too.

'Daddy,' said Jimmy. 'Gran said it wouldn't be a very good garden for growing cabbages. But she said you would like these.'

He gave Dad the white packet. It had 'Marigolds' written on it.

Prayer

Let us think this morning about our families and friends and all the people who care for us.

Hymn
'The family of man' (*Come and Praise* No 69)

Information for the teacher
1   A useful theme for discussion might be 'making the most of what we have'.

2   Interesting follow-up work could focus on growing things – when, why and how do things grow; planting things in gardens, window-boxes – even in the classroom.

The magic bottle   *People*

Introduction
If you were to go to a town in Italy called Genoa, you would find a very big church there. In this church there is a green bottle. People tell a strange story about this bottle. The story starts a long, long time ago when the bottle was owned by a King.

Story
King Umberto sat on his throne and shook the bottle he held in his hand. The bottle was green and he could see some liquid swirling about inside it.

'You see this?' he said to his wife, the Queen. 'This bottle is full of magic liquid – just a drop will keep a dying man alive for years.'

'Indeed,' said the queen. 'Well, my dear, one of your greatest soldiers could do with some of that magic liquid. He has fought many battles for you, but now he is old and dying. Some of that liquid could keep him alive to see his grandchildren.'

'Nonsense,' said the King. 'I'm keeping this liquid for something really special.'

'Oh dear,' sighed the Queen. She knew it was no good arguing with her stubborn and selfish husband.

About a month later a young man who worked for the King was badly kicked whilst he was cleaning the King's horse.

'He is going to die,' said the King's doctor. 'The only thing that could save him would be a drop of the magic liquid in your green bottle.'

'Certainly not,' replied the King. 'That liquid can only be used for somebody who really deserves it.'

Some time later the prime minister of the country became very ill. Over the years he had given King Umberto lots of very good advice and he had always thought the King was his friend.

'Your majesty,' he croaked through dry lips. 'If I am going to stay alive and be any good to you I'll have to have a drop of that magic liquid'.

'I'm afraid not,' said the King. 'That liquid can only be used on a very special occasion.'

The prime minister died. Now the people in the kingdom knew something for certain. The King was keeping the magic liquid in the green bottle for himself – and nobody else.

The years passed by. Then, one day, the King himself became ill. He got worse and worse and then, one morning, he propped himself up in bed and said to his servants, 'Bring me the green bottle'.

The servants looked at each other – and then one of them went off to bring the bottle. When he arrived back with it the King snatched it from his hands. Unscrewing the cork he tipped the bottle to his lips . . . but nothing came out!

The bottle had been kept for so long that all the magic liquid inside it had dried up. With a look of horror at his discovery the King gasped and died.

Afterwards people said that if the King had *shared* the magic liquid from his bottle it would never have run out. By being so selfish he had failed to save other people – and had finally been unable to save himself.

(adapted from an old Italian folk tale)

Prayer

In our prayers this morning, let us remember that people are like bottles. It is not what they look like but what is inside them which really counts.

Hymn

'The best gift' (*Come and Praise* No 59)

Information for the teacher

1   An interesting sideline to this story is to note how important skin bottles were to the people of Jesus' time. These were made by removing hides from animals (eg goats, cows) and then drying them out very slowly. Even today skin bottles are still used in Jerusalem when men carrying them distribute drinks during periods of drought.

2   An old Tibetan saying fits in well with this story: 'The greatest wealth consists of being charitable.'

3   A beautiful book containing more Italian tales is *Italian folk tales* by Italo Clavino (Dent, 1975).

The traveller

Introduction

Sometimes we feel worried when we meet people who are different from us. If they are ill or handicapped we might even be a little frightened of them.

Many years ago when a person had a disease called leprosy everybody kept right away from him in case they caught the disease. Nobody bothered to think about how lepers might feel, or how upset they might be by this treatment. This morning's story is about a leper, a cruel joke, and a brave, kind man.

Story

Guru Nanak was tired. He had walked many miles and when the shadows were made long by the setting sun he was glad to see a village ahead.

It was almost dark when he reached the first house in the village. He knocked on the door. Two young men answered his knock.

'I have travelled far and I would like to stay in your village for the night,' said Guru Nanak. 'Is there someone here who would let me share his house for a night?'

'Hmm, you are a stranger in these parts aren't you?' asked one of the young men.

'Yes', replied the Guru.

'Well then,' said the young man, 'go down into the village until you come to the last house on the right. It's a little way away from the others. It belongs to a man called Nuri – he'll be pleased to put you up for the night.'

'Thank you,' said the Guru. Then a strange thing happened. As he turned to leave, he heard the two young men laughing as they closed the door.

A few minutes later Guru Nanak was standing in front of Nuri's door. He knocked. After a short pause the door opened a little way. Even though it was nearly dark the Guru could still see terrible leprosy scars on the face of the man who opened the door. But he ignored them.

'Good evening, sir,' he said. 'I have been told that you would be kind enough to let me spend the night at your house.'

There was a long pause. For several moments only the sounds of the jungle could be heard in the hot night air. Then Nuri stepped out of his house.

'Look at me, my friend,' he said to Guru Nanak, holding out his diseased arms. 'I am a leper. Nobody wants to come near me, let alone spend a night in my house. I'm afraid the villagers have played a cruel joke on both of us.'

Guru Nanak put his hand on Nuri's shoulder.

'You may be a leper, but you are also a man. May I stay the night with you?'

There was another pause, and the light of the rising moon shone on the tears which glistened in Nuri's eyes.

'Please come in my friend, you are more than welcome.'

The next morning the villagers were astonished when the Guru came out of Nuri's house, where he had obviously spent the night. They were even more astonished as the two men said a fond farewell to each other.

After that the Guru went on his way, but the story did not end there. By some miracle Nuri was cured of leprosy and lived on for many more years in the village. Neither he nor anybody else there ever forgot the night Guru Nanak came – and showed what it meant to be kind.

(adapted from a Sikh story)

Prayer
Let us think this morning about people who are handicapped in some way. Let us remember that just as their bodies may have suffered, their thoughts and feelings can also be hurt by thoughtless or unkind words and deeds.

Hymn
'A man for all people' (*Come and Praise* No 27)

Information for the teacher
1   It is obviously important to tell the children that, with modern medicine, leprosy can now be cured.

2   Sikhs live mostly in the Punjab area of northern India. The word *Sikh* means disciple; all Sikhs are disciples of Guru Nanak who lived from 1469 to 1538. *Guru* means leader or teacher.

3   Useful comparison could be made here with Jesus' attitude to lepers, and the various gospel accounts of curing leprosy: Matthew 8: 1–4; Mark 1: 40–45; Luke 17: 11–19.

Quick thinking   *People*

Introduction
'Help!' Everybody knows what that means – and if we hear it shouted suddenly we might have to do some quick thinking. This morning's story is about a van driver. He was driving along a town street when he heard a cry for help – and he thought, and acted, very quickly indeed.

Story
One morning Cliff Stanton was driving his bread lorry as usual. Suddenly, two women joggers ran right out into the road and Cliff slammed on his

brakes. When he wound his window down he heard the joggers shouting at him.

'Help, help!' one of them cried. 'There's a house on fire round this corner – and there are some children trapped upstairs.'

'OK,' Cliff shouted back. He swung his van round the corner and saw the house which was ablaze. He could hear screams coming from one of the windows upstairs.

'There's only one thing to do,' muttered Cliff, thinking quickly. Turning his van across the road he put it into reverse gear and then began to go backwards as fast as he could.

With a bump the van mounted the pavement, then there was a loud crash as it broke through the fence surrounding the burning house.

'So far so good,' thought Cliff as he continued to drive the van backwards over the lawn and the flowers. Then, when the back of his van was right next to the house, he shouted from the cab to the children upstairs.

'Jump!' shouted Cliff. 'You'll be all right. You haven't far to fall – just onto the top of this van.'

Slowly the upstairs window opened, and a little boy jumped out. He landed quite safely on top of the van and a neighbour who had just arrived, helped him down to the ground.

A little girl jumped next, and then another little girl. Eventually all the children, and two grown ups, got out of the burning house by jumping on top of the van. Soon the fire brigade arrived and set about putting the fire out.

Some time later Mr Jim Carty said that his nine children and two grandchildren had all been saved by Mr Stanton's quick thinking.

'We are all very, very grateful to Cliff Stanton,' said Mr Carty.

Prayer
Let us give thanks for those ordinary people who act quickly without thought for themselves, and by their actions save the lives of others.

Hymn
'Travel on' (*Come and Praise* No 42)

Information for the teacher
This incident took place in Birkenhead, Merseyside. Cliff Stanton was driving a 16 ton van and only one of the people he rescued was hurt. This was a 13-year-old boy who fell between the back of the van and the house wall as he was escaping from the bedroom. Although he had to be taken to hospital his injuries were only minor.

'Let's enjoy a good story' *People*

Introduction
Can you imagine what it was like before there was any television? Well, one of the things which people enjoyed then was listening to stories. This morning we are going to hear about a man who told marvellous stories. He lived about a hundred years ago and his name was Sabine.

Story
A long time ago a man called Sabine lived in a small village in Yorkshire. He was better off than most of the other people who lived in the village and he saw how hard both grown ups and children had to work.

'It would be nice if they had something to look forward to at the end of their day's work,' thought Sabine to himself. 'I wonder . . .'

Now one of the things that Sabine was good at was telling stories. He always seemed to find just the right words to make his stories exciting.

'That's what I'll do,' he thought. 'I'll start telling stories in my house at night, and anybody who wants to, can come and listen.'

A few days later news got around about what was going to happen. One cold, wet night two men, two ladies and three children turned up at Sabine's house. He asked them in and soon they were listening, fascinated, to one of his stories. The next day at work others asked what it had been like.

'What happened at the story teller's?'

'It was great – you should come along.'

'Did many people go?'

'Not really, there is plenty of room.'

The next night Sabine's front room was more crowded and again the listeners to his stories went away very pleased. They told their friends how good the stories were, and more people started to come.

'I'd never have believed this!' said Sabine a few days later. Now, when they had finished work, crowds of grown ups and children flocked to his house. They packed into his front room, crowded into the kitchen, and even sat on the stairs to listen.

'I'm glad they enjoy the stories,' thought Sabine. 'I'm sure they would enjoy singing too when they are all together. I know what I'll do, I'll write a special hymn that we can all sing before everybody goes home.'

So Sabine wrote some words and music and every night after that the sound of singing could be heard coming from his little house.

Soon after this, Sabine left Yorkshire and went to live in Devon. Here he started to write books and, before he died, he had written one hundred and fifity of them. But the people of the little village of Horbury Brig in Yorkshire never forgot their favourite story teller.

Prayer

This morning's prayer uses some of the words which Sabine wrote for the people to sing after they had listened to his stories:

> Now the day is over,
> Night is drawing nigh,
> Shadows of the evening
> Steal across the sky.
>
> Now the darkness gathers,
> Stars beging to peep,
> Birds and beasts and flowers
> Soon will be asleep.

Sabine Baring-Gould

Hymn

'I listen and I listen' (*Come and Praise* No 60)

Information for the teacher

1   'Now the day is over' is not in *Come and Praise*, but can be found in many hymn anthologies. One of these is *With Cheerful Voice* (A and C Black 1966) – it includes a simple melody line for children's use.

2   'Sabine' was the Rev Sabine Baring-Gould, who lived from 1834 to 1924. He also wrote 'Onward Christian Soldiers'.

3   The value and power of stories is obviously recognised by all religions and cultures. Alan T Dale says: 'The clear intention of Jesus was to call everybody to fearless thought as well as splendid living.'

   His book '*New World – The Heart of the New Testament in Plain English*' (Oxford University Press 1967) remains one of the very best for New Testament story adaptations, and many of these can be used with infants.

The soldier who would not fight   *People*

Introduction

This morning's story is an unusual one. It is about a soldier who would not fight. He did not believe in hurting people so he would not fire any guns. His job was to help wounded soldiers.

   The amazing thing about this story is that, in spite of not fighting, this soldier won the highest medal his country could give. This is what happened.

Story

Desmond was an American soldier. In a terrible war America was fighting Japan. Both American and Japanese soldiers were on an island. Each side wanted to capture the island.

Desmond had asked if he could go to where the fighting was at its worst and there were many wounded men who needed his help.

'You've got a lot to do here Desmond,' shouted the captain. '75 of my men are wounded and need to go to hospital.'

'OK captain,' replied Desmond. 'I'll carry them down to where the ambulances are waiting.'

So, with a friend, Desmond carried the 75 men to where the ambulances were waiting. Then he reported back to the captain.

'Out there,' said the captain, 'are four more wounded men.'

He pointed across a field to where four men lay still in the crumpled grass. Bullets whistled all round and there was a tremendous noise.

'I'm on my way,' said Desmond.

Jumping to his feet he dodged in and out of the flying bullets until he reached the first man.

'We'll soon have you out of here,' said Desmond, as he took some bandages out of the bag he carried. Skilfully he tied a bandage round the injured man's leg. Then, lifting him on his back he ran back to the safety of the American trenches.

Once he knew the man was safe Desmond went back to each of the others in turn. Bandaging them up he carried them to safety.

'Great work Desmond,' said the captain, 'but I'm afraid there is another wounded man out there now'.

Picking up his bag of bandages Desmond dashed over the field once again. He had almost reached the wounded man when he felt a sudden pain in his leg.

'I'm hit!' he thought, but he staggered on until he reached the other soldier.

'You'll soon be OK,' said Desmond, bandaging the other man's wounds.

'But . . . you're hurt too,' said the soldier, 'your leg . . . look at it.'

No sooner had he spoken than another bullet hit Desmond in the arm. Now he was more badly wounded than the man he had come to help. Meanwhile the captain had seen what was happening and he sent out two men with a stretcher. When they reached Desmond and the other wounded man Desmond spoke to them.

'Right, get this poor fellow onto that stretcher and get him to safety,' he said. Soon the wounded soldier was rushed away. Desmond started to crawl back to the American trenches. He was in awful pain and he had just reached safety when he fainted. Soon everybody had heard about Desmond's great courage and determination to help others.

'This man deserves a medal', said the President of the United States of America, 'and he shall have one.'

When Desmond recovered from his wounds the President gave him a medal. It is called the Medal of Honour and it is the most important medal anybody in America can win.

Prayer

Lead me from Death to Life; from Falsehood to Truth.
Lead me from Despair to Hope; from Fear to Trust.
Lead me from Hate to Love; from War to Peace.
Let Peace fill our Heart, our World, our Universe.
Peace, Peace, Peace.

(The Prayer for Peace)

Hymn

'Peace, perfect peace' (*Come and Praise* No 53)

Information for the teacher

1   'Desmond' was Private First Class Desmond T Doss. Due to his courage at the battle for Okinawa in 1945 he was awarded the Medal of Honour. The presentation was made by President Truman on 12 October 1945.

2   The Prayer for Peace was first announced at St James Church, Piccadilly by Mother Teresa in 1981. Nine months later at the Assembly of World Religions it was said by 900 delegates. It has since been translated into more than 400 languages.

Mother Teresa was born in Yugoslavia on 17 August, 1910. She went to India in 1948 to be a teacher. She was so shocked by the poverty and suffering she saw on the streets of Calcutta that she decided to dedicate the rest of her life to helping the sufferers. She is now world famous and much medicine, money and other gifts have been sent to help her Mission of Charity. She herself remains a very humble person – 'I do nothing, Jesus does it all'.

The three brothers   *People*

Introduction

This morning's story is about three brothers in a far-off land long, long ago. Their names were Ivan, Alex and Boris. One day they all left home to seek their fortunes.

Story

'Well my brothers,' said Ivan, 'here we are beneath the story tree outside the village.'

Alex and Boris nodded. Everybody knew about the story tree because it was where the villagers gathered on hot summer evenings to gossip and tell stories.

'Let's go our separate ways from here,' went on Ivan, 'and meet at this exact spot, at this exact time, five years from now. Then we'll see how each of us has done.'

Alex and Boris nodded again and then the three of them set off on their separate ways.

Now Ivan was a very hard working man and good with his hands. He settled in a village and began to make tables and chairs, cradles and chests. Soon he was known as the best carpenter around and he began to earn quite a lot of money. He saved up a bag of gold coins to show his brothers how well he had done.

Alex went to a town. There he got a stall in a market. Soon he was buying and selling clothes and making a good living. He too began to save gold coins in a bag to show his brothers.

Boris meanwhile had wandered off into the country. He liked the feel of fresh air on his face, and he enjoyed watching the sun cast its shadows on the hills and valleys. Soon he came upon a shepherd with a flock of sheep. The shepherd was an old man and was delighted when Boris asked if he could help. Five years passed quickly and Boris enjoyed every minute of being a shepherd. Then he remembered the meeting with his brothers. He told the old shepherd the story.

'Hmm,' said the shepherd. 'You've got to show them how you've made your fortune have you? Well, my friend, we have no money – only our flock of sheep. To be rich we'd have to sell our sheep.'

'No, no,' said Boris. 'They're your sheep. I wouldn't dream of taking any.'

'You're a kind lad,' said the old shepherd, 'and I would like to give you a gift to show you how much I have enjoyed being your friend. Please take this.'

So saying, the old man handed Boris his shepherd's staff. Boris took the smooth, well-worn piece of wood and smoothed his hand down it.

'Thank you,' he said.

The day came for the three brothers to meet again. Beneath the story tree they came upon each other, shook hands and slapped each other on the back. Then Ivan showed his bag of gold coins, and Alex showed *his* bag of gold coins.

'Come on little brother, what have you got?' they both asked Boris.

'Well, I've had five wonderful years,' said Boris, 'and my old friend the shepherd very kindly gave me his staff.'

At first Ivan and Alex looked at him in amazement. Then they laughed. Then they said angrily. 'He's made you work for nothing. You've been a fool.'

Boris was upset and sad. Leaving his brothers he wandered off. He sat down on a rock and thought of the kind old man, of how much he enjoyed being a shepherd, and how getting bags of gold coins didn't seem to matter very much. Then, as he stood up, he gave the rock an absent-minded tap with his staff. At once an amazing thing happened. With a great cracking noise the rock opened and, one by one, out of it came dozens and dozens of sheep.

Boris couldn't believe his eyes. Now he understood that the old man's gift had been worth far more than bags of gold coins.

Prayer
Let us pray this morning that when we grow up we can find happiness and contentment in the jobs we do.

Hymn
'A man for all the people' (*Come and Praise* No 27)

Information for the teacher
Shepherds feature greatly in the Bible and a few incidental pieces of information about them might be useful discussion points in connection with this assembly, eg:

- the sheep's greatest enemy was the snake;
- the shepherd's staff was used to lift and guide sheep on dangerous and rocky routes;
- shepherds wore a hooded cloak (*abayeh*) which protected them from all weathers, and made a voluminous shelter at night. It often lasted a lifetime;
- shepherds carried pebbles and threw them to attract the sheep's attention;
- shepherds usually carried food for several days in a bag – cheese, bread, raisins, olives, and a water bottle;
- shepherds often had dogs and played reed pipes when resting;

(Useful Biblical references: John 10:11; Isiah 40:11; Psalm 78: 70–72.)

The quarrel   *People*

Introduction
All of us have quarrels and arguments at some time or another. Perhaps the only good thing about an argument is when it is over and people become

friends again. Sometimes, however, quarrels go on for a very, very long time. Nobody will say, 'Sorry, let's be friends again' so the two people often get even more sulky and unfriendly.

This morning we are going to listen to a poem instead of a story. It is about two boys who were very good friends. That is, until they bought a bike between them – and started arguing about who should use it.

Poem

The Quarrel

It was a joint partnership.
They owned this bike
And they argued over it,
'I should have it, right?'

'It's my turn,' shouted Tom,
'Didn't you have it last night?'
'No, you had it.'
Then the quarrel turned into a fight.

One night over by the disco,
Down near County Hall,
They had one almighty battle,
And both ended up in hospital.

The bike had stood
In Joe's old shed next door,
And until the argument was over
It was used no more.

This went on for
A year and a day,
And when they next looked at the bike,
It had rusted away.

So no more did they argue,
They just sat on the wood,
And stared at the place
Where their bike once stood.

Mark Winyard

Prayer

Perhaps one reason why a person quarrels is because he or she is lonely and unhappy. Let us be glad that most of us have somebody we can turn to for help . . . .

> **Do your agree?**
> I couldn't bear to think
> that
> there wasn't
> anybody
> anywhere
> who cared, just a bit
> about me.
> I couldn't bear to think
> that
> there wasn't
> somebody
> somewhere
> who shared my hopes,
> my fears,
> my joy,
> my tears.
>
> S Simpson

Hymn

'God knows me' (*Come and Praise* No 15)

Information for the teacher

More reasons why people quarrel could be discussed – prejudice, greed, stubbornness, envy etc. There are many Biblical references to quarrels and the following could be useful:

Luke 7, 1–10 (overcoming hate); Luke 10, 25–37 (overcoming racial prejudice); Luke 18, 18–33 (overcoming greed); Luke 15, 11–32 (overcoming stubbornness); Mark 3, 1–6 (overcoming envy).

The red cap   *People*

Introduction

This morning's story is about a little boy called David. He had a bright red cap and he liked to wear it all the time – he even tried to go to bed in it!

David lived beside some very deep water which was called a canal. He and his friend John were both four years old. They often used to play beside this canal, and of course David always had his bright red cap on.

Story

'Come on David,' shouted John one day, 'let's go and play beside the canal.'

'Great,' replied David, and the two boys ran off to play beside the water.

'Let's play spacemen,' said John.

'OK,' replied David.

The two boys began to chase up and down the canal bank playing spacemen. Neither of them noticed a big brick which was lying in the grass.

'Bet you can't catch me,' shouted David, as he raced along the bank. Then, suddenly, his foot caught the brick and he fell forward with a splash, straight into the canal!

'David, David!' yelled John. David was in the water, he couldn't swim, and he was already beginning to sink. The bright red cap floated near him.

'Help, help!' John ran along the bank shouting as loudly as he could.

'What is it?' shouted Donna, David's older sister, who was ten.

'It's David,' yelled John. 'He's fallen in the water.'

'What!' cried Donna.

'He needs help,' shouted John.

Quickly Donna, and her sister Helen who was eight, raced back to their house.

'Dad,' gasped Donna. 'David's fallen in the canal. Come quickly.'

Mr Cotton, the girls' and David's father, leapt out of his chair and raced down to the canal. He saw John standing crying by the side of the water, but there was no sign of David.

'David, David!' shouted Mr Cotton.

There was no reply. Then he saw something bobbing on top of the water. It was a red cap.

'He must be under there somewhere,' thought Mr Cotton. He dived into the canal and began swimming in the dark and dirty water. Suddenly Mr Cotton saw a shape in the mud. It was David. Mr Cotton reached out for the boy and began to pull him to the surface of the water.

With a great gasp Mr Cotton burst into the sunlight. David did not move. Swimming quickly to the bank Mr Cotton dragged himself out, pulling David with him. Stretching him out on the grass Mr Cotton gave his son the kiss of life. After a few minutes David gave a long cough, and began to breathe again. He was going to be all right!

Later, when he was completely better, David thought how lucky he had been to have a good friend with him, and a brave father to rescue him. He is always very, very careful when he plays beside the canal now.

(adapted from a Sunday newspaper report)

Prayer
Let us think this morning about how the floating red cap helped to show where David was. Let us pray that we can notice signs that people need help – are miserable, lonely or tired. Let us pray that we can help people in whatever way is best.

Hymn
'O praise ye the Lord' (*Come and Praise* No 37)

Information for the teacher
1   It is obviously important to point out that children as young as four should not be playing near water without supervision.

2   A possible follow up to this story could be more work on 'signs' – Red cross for help, nurses' uniform, red for danger etc.

3   As an example of physical bravery this story could be compared with similar stories of courage in the Bible, eg: 1 Samuel 17: 34–35 fight with wild animals; 2 Samuel 23: 15–17 braving danger to get water for a leader; Luke 10: 30–34 the Samaritan's bravery; Acts 27: 18–25 Paul's courage in a storm.

4   Display the following from *The Blue Code for Water Safety*; issued by the Royal Life Saving Society, Mountbatten House, Studley, Warks B80 7NN. Tel: (052 785) 3943.
- If someone else falls in, *don't go in the water after him*;
- Don't panic;
- Look for something to help pull him out – stick, rope, clothing;
- Lie down to prevent yourself being pulled in;
- If you cannot reach him, throw any floating object e.g. a football, plastic bottle – for him to hold on to, then *fetch help*.

Raksha Bandhan   *People*

Introduction
Many of us have brothers and sisters and sometimes we just take them for granted without thinking too much about it. Today's assembly, however, is about a very special day for brothers and sisters.

Story
Dipti and Jigme were very excited. Today was the day Mrs Thomas had said they could tell the rest of the class all about Raksha Bandhan. When the

twins got to school the register was soon called and then Mrs Thomas spoke to the class.

'Now children, today Dipti and Jigme are going to tell us all about a special day for brothers and sisters. Sit very quietly and listen to what they have to say.'

Dipti came out to the front of the class.

'Good morning everybody,' she said. 'One of the days I like best in the whole year is called Raksha Bandhan, and I am going to tell you why. When I get up I find that my Mum has left some red and gold thread out for me. It is bright and sparkly and looks lovely. I get the thread and go to where my Mum and Dad and Jigme are waiting for me.

'Have you got the Rakhi?' my Mum usually asks. The Rakhi is the proper name for the red and gold thread I have told you about.

Next I get hold of Jigme's hands one at a time and I tie the Rakhi round each wrist. When I have done this Jigme looks as if he has got bracelets of red and gold thread on. As I do the tying Mum usually says to me: "Remember the prayer, Dipti."

This is to remind me that as I tie the thread I must say a little prayer asking for my brother to be always safe and protected.'

'That's very interesting Dipti,' said Mrs Thomas when Dipti had stopped speaking, 'but what about you Jigme? Can you tell us what it is like for you on this very special day?'

'Oh it's great,' said Jigme. 'When Dipti ties the thread on my wrists I make a promise.'

'What is that?' asked Mrs Thomas.

'Well, just as Dipti has said a prayer asking for me to be safe and protected, I promise that no matter what happens I will always look after my sister.'

'Thank you both,' said Mrs Thomas, and Dipti and Jigme went back to their seats. 'I think we should all remember the day of Raksha Bandhan when brothers and sisters think especially about looking after and caring for each other.'

Prayer
Let us pray this morning for our brothers and sisters. Let us be grateful for the fact that there are people who love us and care about us.

Hymn
'The building song' (*Come and Praise* No 61)

Information for the teacher
Raksha Bandhan is a Hindu festival which reminds brothers and sisters of their responsibilities. It is held once a year on the full moon of Sharavan.

(As this usually falls in our calendar month of August, commemoration of the actual anniversary is impossible in school time, but the story can be used at any time in the school year).

The tradition behind the festival is that Indra's wife was given some red and gold thread by the great god Vishnu. By tying it around Indra's wrist she was able to protect him from the evil king Bali.

The word Raksha means 'to protect' and the word Bandhan means 'to tie.' For more details about Indra look for the collection of Hindu hymns called the *Rig Vedu* which tells of his influence, power and personality.

Enough for two   *People*

Introduction
There once lived a very famous man called Muhammad. To help people see that it is better to be kind than unkind he told them stories.

This morning we are going to hear about a very thirsty man and a very thirsty dog. They both lived in a hot country where there wasn't much water.

Story
Anwar was hot! He was so hot that he could think of nothing else but water. If only he could get a drink to wet his dry, parched mouth. Slowly he dragged one foot after the other across the dusty road. Then he saw another well by the roadside a short distance ahead.

'I expect it's like the last two,' he thought. Within the last few miles he had come across two wells but both had been dry.

Slowly he approached the third well. Lying beside it was a dog. Its bones were almost sticking through its sides it was so thin. Its tongue was hanging out and it was breathing in gasps.

'Get out of my way,' said Anwar, who was desperate to see if the well had any water in it. As he got nearer he could see that there was no bucket, no rope to wind down, no handle to do the winding. That was a bad start! Reaching the edge of the well he peered down into it. He could see nothing. Then, bending down, he picked up a pebble and dropped it into the well. For a second there was silence, then 'Plop!'

'Water!' gasped Anwar. Putting his leg over the wall he began to climb down into the well. It was very difficult because all the time he had to hang on by his fingers and toes. Eventually however he reached the bottom – and it was all worth it.

'This is marvellous,' he said out loud as he stood waist deep in cool, clean water. He poured it over his head, threw it on his chest and drank great, deep mouthfuls of it. Then, feeling a new man, he climbed back up out of the well. As he stood dripping and refreshed beside the wall at the top he heard a pitiful whine. There, staggering towards him and trying to lick up the drops of water which had fallen from his clothes, Anwar saw the dog.

'Look at him,' he thought. 'He is as desperate for a drink as I was, but he can't climb to get one.'

Then Anwar had an idea. Turning, he slid back over the wall and climbed down the well once again. When he reached the bottom he took off one of his boots and filled it with water. Then, clenching the water-filled boot tightly between his teeth he climbed up and out again. Setting the boot down in front of the dog, Anwar watched as the poor creature drank thirstily. When it had finished it looked up at Anwar and the expression in its eyes made all his efforts seem worthwhile.

Prayer
Let us think this morning about how doing a kind deed often means making a great deal of effort. Let us remember the story of Anwar so that we too are always prepared to do so much as is necessary to be kind.

Hymn
'Fill thou my life' (*Come and Praise* No 41)

Information for the teacher
1   This Muslim story might also be linked to a special occasion assembly, taking note of Eid-ul-Fitr. For Muslim children this is one of the most memorable festivals, when the end of the month-long fast of Ramadan is celebrated with a party atmosphere.

   A very attractive little book on Eid-ul-Fitr can be found in the *Celebrations* series published by Ginn.

2   Jesus also used stories or *parables* to convey his message, making it easier for ordinary people to understand.

3   In societies where many people could not read or write, story-telling was very important – both as a form of entertainment and a means of passing on traditional wisdom.

The long walk   *People*

Introduction
What happens when your shoe gets a hole in it? Probably your mum or dad takes it to the cobbler's and the cobbler mends it.

Luckily we don't get holes in our shoes very often, but this morning's story is about a man called Dennison Berwick who had to have his shoes mended 50 times in seven months. That means he had to have his shoes mended twice, or more, every week!

'He must have done a lot of walking' you might be saying to yourselves – and you would be right. This is his story.

Story

Dennison Berwick had heard about poor children who live in India. He felt very sorry for them.

'They seem to have more awful things happening to them than most,' he thought. 'They hardly ever have enough to eat; many can't go to school; often they are not properly cared for when they are ill. I wonder how I might help?'

Dennison thought about this for a long time and then he came to a decision. 'I'll do a sponsored walk,' he thought. 'I'll ask people to give some money for every mile I walk. Then I will give the money I have collected to an organisation that helps poor children in India.'

Dennison decided to give the money to Save the Children Fund, a group of people who try to help those in need.

What he said next gave his mother a shock!

'I'm not going to walk in England, Mum,' he said. 'I'm going to India and I'm going to walk along the whole distance of their great river, the River Ganges. That way I'll be able to see lots of the children I'm raising money for.'

Dennison got on an areoplane and flew thousands of miles to India. When he got there the first thing he noticed was how hot it was.

'This is going to be a very hard country to walk in,' he thought. 'I'm going to get very, very hot and tired.'

Then he set off on his long walk. He started at the seaside, where the River Ganges met the sea. He wore as few clothes as possible, and sandals on his feet. After walking for hours in the burning sun he felt as if he must have a rest.

'That'll be a good spot – under that tree,' he thought. 'It will be cooler there because I'll be in the shade.'

Puffing his cheeks out and blowing some air onto his face, Dennison slumped down in the shade of the tree. Immediately his left foot began to itch, then his leg, then his arm. He was covered with ants and flies! What's more, they all seemed to want to bite him at the same time.

'This is going to be worse than I thought,' Dennison said to himself. But brushing away the insects he started walking again.

Day after day Dennison kept at it. At first he thought he wouldn't be able to stand the heat, but gradually he got used to it. Then he reached higher ground and it began to get a little cooler. Now, however, it was harder work because he was climbing all the time.

Week after week went by and then, seven months after he had started, Dennison reached the end of the River Ganges.

'I've made it!' he shouted to anybody who would listen. He felt tired but delighted. His long, long sponsored walk was over and that meant he could now collect £10 000 to help the poor children of India.

Prayer

> Do all the good you can,
> By all the means you can,
> In all the ways you can,
> In all the places you can,
> At all the times you can,
> To all the people you can,
> As long as ever you can.
>
> John Wesley

Hymn
'Travel on' (*Come and Praise* No 42)

Information for the teacher

1   Dennison actually walked 1557 miles. The temperature on the Plains reached 117°F; on his final stretch he climbed 12 000 feet into the Himalayas. On completion of his walk he had had his sandals repaired 50 times and he had lost 30lbs in weight.

2   The Ganges is a holy river to Hindus. They believe that bathing in it will remove their sins. The holy city of Benares (now called Varanasi) stands on the Ganges. Tens of thousands of Hindus go there every year and bathe in the river from the steps (*ghats*) alongside. Many bathers take away bottles of Ganges water to give to those who cannot make the trip.

3   Save the Children Fund have many very useful and informative publications about overseas aid and development projects in India and elsewhere. Their address is:
Save the Children Fund, 157 Clapham Road, London SW9.

4   An excellent book of reference for anything to do with India is: *We live in India* by Brahm Dev (Wayland 1981). The book paints a vivid picture of what it is like to live in India.

All that glitters . . .   *People*

Introduction

This morning's story is rather a sad one. It is about some fishermen who lived long ago in a hot country. For a long time they were happy catching their fish and living with their families and friends in a small village.

Then one day they saw something which made them think they could become very rich. At once they forgot about everything else, all they wanted was the treasure they could see – or thought they could see. This is their story.

Story

'There it is again,' said one of the fishermen, leaning over the side of the boat. 'Look.'

The others gazed down into the sea. Deep down they saw the flashing of beautiful colours.

'There must be jewels down there,' said the first fisherman. 'If we bring them up we'll be rich. We won't need to be simple fishermen any more.'

For the rest of the day they gave up any thought of fishing and dived in one after the other to try and reach the jewels. But no matter how far down they went, they could not reach whatever it was that glinted and gleamed so beautifully. Finally they gave up and rowed ashore.

'There is only one way to get those jewels,' said one of the fishermen that night as they sat round the fire, feeling rather hungry because they had not caught enough fish to eat. 'We'll have to tie something heavy to our feet so that we can get right down to the ocean floor. Then we can pick up the jewels, throw off the weights, and swim back to the surface.'

The next day the fishermen set out to sea again. In their boat they had some large rocks and some tough creepers. The sun shone brilliantly overhead and, sure enough, the fishermen saw the jewels glinting below.

Carefully the fishermen tied the heavy rocks to their feet with the stringy, tough creepers. With a big splash the first of them went over the side. The heavy rock dragged him down quickly. The minutes passed . . .

After a while one of the others said what they were all thinking.

'He should be back by now.'

'Perhaps he's come to the surface somewhere else.'

'No – we would have seen him.'

'Let's all go down and find him, and the jewels.'

So, with the heavy weights tied to their feet, the rest of the fishermen jumped one by one into the sea. Down and down they went to search for the treasure which was going to make them all rich.

Hours later the fishing boat still rocked gently on the calm, sunlit sea. None of the fishermen returned to tell of their search for the jewels. Of course there were no jewels – just a sunbeam which flashed and glittered deep down in the calm sea.

Prayer
Let us think this morning about the fact that what something looks like does not always tell us what it is worth. It is the same with people, what they say and think and do is much more important than how they look. Let us pray that we will learn not to judge by appearances.

Hymn
'For the beauty of the earth' (*Come and Praise* No 11)

Information for the teacher
1   An apt quotation here is: 'Be on your guard against greed of every kind, for even when a man has more than enough, his wealth does not give him life.'

   Useful Biblical references on a similar theme are: Mark 10: 17–30; Luke 12: 13–21; Mark 12: 41–44.

2   A useful parallel story about the vanity of earthly treasure is told in Luke 12: 16–20. It tells of the rich farmer who built bigger and better barns to store up all his wheat and wealth, so that he could concentrate on nothing but enjoyment. No sooner had he done this than he died.

3   A third possibility would be to link this story with that of Midas – and the consequences of his wish for gold. A lovely book for infants, which tells the Midas story simply and with good illustrations, is *King Midas and the Golden Touch* (an *I can read by myself* book) published by Collins and Harvill, 1970.

Growing up   *People*

Introduction
Put your hands up, those of you who are eight. Keep your hands up if you can remember something which happened to you when you were seven. (Pause for comments here, then repeat – with seven-year-olds remembering incidents when they were six and so on.)

   Most of us remember things that happened when we were younger. Now listen to this poem.

Poem

Can't wait

Not having much fun
At One.

In a cage (like a zoo)
At Two.

Scraping a knee
At Three.

Ever asking for more
At Four.

Busy bee in a hive
At Five.

Playing war with sticks
At Six.

Running is heaven
At Seven.

I can't wait
To be Eight.

John Kitching

The thing about getting older is that we get bigger and stronger and we are supposed to get more sense as we do so. We should learn to think about other people as well as ourselves; we should learn how we can help each other at home and at school; we should learn to try our hardest at whatever we do.

The poem we have listened to reminds us of the *fun* of growing up. The prayer which follows reminds us of the *importance* of growing up.

Prayer

Let us think this morning of growing stronger and learning more. Let us think of how we can learn from our mothers and fathers, older brothers and sisters, teachers and friends, as we grow. Let us try to become kinder and more thoughtful people ourselves.

Hymn

'The family of man' (*Come and Praise* No 69)

Information for the teacher

1   A relevant Bible quotation might be: 'Train up a child in the way he should go and when he is old he will not depart from it.' (Proverbs 22:6)

2   Some health notes on 'growing up' might be useful in this assembly. For example, a baby is born with some abilities – sucking, swallowing, stretching, grasping etc – but must learn everything else, usually from the mother. Physical growth requires the correct intake of proteins, fats, carbohydrates, minerals.

3   In connection with the last point, this a good opportunity to make comparisons between the expected growth of a child in a normal British school, and that of a deprived child in the Third World.

4   Useful reference material: *Human Body* from the Sampson Low *New Horizon Library*; and material from organisations such as
Christian Aid, 240 Ferndale Road, London SW9 8BH
Oxfam, 274 Banbury Road, Oxford.

The greedy brother   *People*

Introduction

This morning's story took place in a far-off land, long ago. It is about two brothers. One of them was kind and friendly and his name was Hussain. The other was sly and greedy and his name was Abdul. This is what happened to them.

Story

Hussain was very sad. His father and mother had just died.

'What a very sad time this is,' Hussain said to his brother Abdul.

'Hmm,' replied Abdul. 'I'm afraid our parents did not leave very much. There is just the house – which I will live in, of course – that bit of land under the mountain, and the cat and the dog. You can have them.'

'Thank you,' said Hussain. Now he did not know that his father had left a great deal of money, many rice fields and lots of oxen to pull the carts. Abdul had stolen all these things without letting his brother know.

The next day Hussain went to plough the land near the mountain.

'Oh dear,' he thought, 'the only animals I have to pull the plough are the cat and the dog. I suppose they will have to do.'

So there he was, following a plough being pulled by a cat and a dog. The Lord of the Mountain was watching from high above the field. When he saw this ridiculous sight he opened his mouth wide to roar with laughter. As he did so a huge split in the mountain opened – showing a great store of gold inside.

Hussain saw the gold glinting in the sunlight. Quickly dashing inside the mountain he filled a sack with the treasure. Then he dived out, just as the Lord of the Mountain finished laughing and closed his mouth.

'Phew, that was close,' said Hussain to himself. 'Still, how lucky I have been. Abdul will be pleased to hear about my good luck.'

When he got home he went to see Abdul and told him the whole story.

'That's wonderful,' said Abdul, 'now you'll be able to build yourself a nice house, and get some oxen to pull the plough. I am very pleased for you.'

All the time he was talking, however, Abdul was plotting. Despite having stolen all the money which had been meant for Hussain as well as himself he was still greedy for more.

'I wonder if I might be as lucky too,' he said to Hussain. 'Will you lend me the dog and the cat so that I can try?'

'Of course', said Hussain 'and good luck.'

Next morning Abdul set out. As well as the dog and cat, he took a huge cart pulled by two oxen; a large pile of sacks; and his wife to help him fill them. Then, hiding everything else, he strapped the dog and cat into the plough and began to work in front of the mountain.

High above the Lord of the Mountain looked down and saw the ridiculous dog and cat ploughing again. Opening his mouth wide he roared with laughter once more. This was the moment Abdul had been waiting for. Seeing the gold as the mountain opened, he shouted to his wife. They dashed inside and began to fill up the sacks as fast as they could.

The Lord of the Mountain went on laughing as one sack was filled, but then he noticed that the two greedy people were filling another . . . and another . . . and . . .

With a roar of anger the Lord of the Mountain stopped laughing and slammed his mouth shut. Abdul and his wife had been so greedy that they had no chance to get out in time, and they were never seen again.

So Hussain got all the land and money which was really his – and Abdul's share as well.

(adapted from *A World of Folk Tales* by J Riordan)

Prayer

Let us pray for a world in which there is less greed and dishonesty.

Hymn
'Go tell it on the mountain' (*Come and Praise* No 24)

Information for the teacher
1   In the Bible the word 'charity' is never used in the sense of giving alms, but rather as another interpretation of 'love'.

2   Two Jewish sayings are appropriate here:
    'The more the charity the more the peace.'
    'True charity is practised in secret. The best type of charity is where the person who gives does not know who receives; and the person who receives does not know who gives.'

The dream   *People*

Introduction
All of us have dreams from time to time. This morning's story is about a little girl who had a dream – and how it came true in the strangest way.

Story
Selwyn, Leon and Roseann were on their way to school. Their mothers had left them at the end of the lane which led to the school gates.

'I had a funny dream last night,' said Roseann.

'Did you dream you were a princess?' asked Selwyn, and he and Leon giggled.

'No, silly,' went on Roseann, 'but I dreamt I found £1 and I used it to buy a birthday present for my mum. Its her birthday on Thursday.'

Just a moment later, Rosean pointed to a muddy patch in the lane just ahead of them. 'Hey, look!' she exclaimed. Lying, squashed in the mud, was a purse.

'I wonder what's inside it?' said Roseann as she pulled the purse out of the mud. Opening it she looked inside. It was full of money – £10 notes, £5 notes, and £1 coins.

'Your dream has come true,' said Leon, 'but you haven't found £1, you've found lots.'

'Don't be silly,' said Roseann, 'this isn't my money. Some poor person has lost it and they will want it back.'

So when the children got to school Roseann gave the purse to Miss Garrett, the headmistress.

'Thank you Roseann,' said Miss Garrett. 'I'll put a notice up by the gate saying that we have somebody's purse here. Perhaps they'll see the notice and come and claim it.'

Roseann didn't think any more about the purse, or her dream. The rest of Monday passed normally, so did Tuesday, and then . . . on Wednesday, Garrett came into the classroom while everybody was painting.

'I'm sorry to interrupt, Miss Martin,' said Miss Garrett, 'but I wonder if I could take Roseann with me for a moment.'

'Of course,' said Miss Martin.

'Come with me Roseann,' said Miss Garrett, and taking Roseann by the hand she went to her office. Inside was a tall, old, grey-haired lady.

'This is Roseann, Mrs Briggs,' said Miss Garrett.

'Oh I'm so pleased to meet you,' said Mrs Briggs. 'It was my purse you found the other day. You know I've just got a new grandson and the money in the purse was to pay my fare to go and see him. Thanks to you I'll be able to go now.'

Roseann blushed and bowed her head. She didn't know what to say.

'I had to see you and thank you for being so honest,' went on Mrs Briggs, 'and I would like you to have this as a little reward.'

Then she held out a £1 coin for Roseann.

'Thank you,' said Roseann. She thought at the same time, 'My dream has come true!'

'I'll be able to buy my mum a birthday present with this,' she said, and both Miss Garrett and Mrs Briggs smiled.

Prayer

Let us give thanks this morning that most people are honest. Let us also pray for those who are tempted not to be and who might keep, or take, things which don't belong to them.

Hymn

'Lost and found'(*Come and Praise* No 57)

Information for the teacher

The Old Testament philosophy that whatever was true was also good and beautiful is certainly a theme which appeals to young children – it is not what you look like, who you are or what you say which is important, but what you do. This story also lends itself very readily to some simple mime or drama.

Fish and chips are nice!   *People*

Introduction

Most of us like everything about fish and chips. They look nice, they smell nice and they taste nice – particularly with tomato sauce on them.

This morning's story is about fish and chips. At first it may seem rather a silly story. That is, until you think about it. Now, I want you to imagine a fish and chip van standing on a corner. People keep going up to it and buying themselves fish and chips. A tasty smell floats all around.

Story

Jock had hardly any money and he was very, very hungry. He'd had no breakfast and he'd saved the slice of bread in his pocket to have for dinner.

'Oh, what I'd give to have some of those fish and chips,' he thought as he stood beside the brightly-painted van, watching people buy their packets of fish and chips.

'I haven't enough money though, so I'll just have to make the most of my slice of bread.'

Getting out the bread Jock bit into it and chewed slowly. All around him floated the lovely smell of the fish and chips – but his dry bread still tasted like dry bread!

Meanwhile Errol, the man in the fish and chip van, had been working hard. He'd made lots of money. But every time he looked up he noticed the poor, thin-looking man eating a slice of bread very slowly.

'It's not fair,' thought Errol. 'Why should he stand there like that? He should pay me.'

'Hey you,' called out Errol to Jock. 'You'd better pay what you owe me.'

'Pay you . . . owe you?' answered Jock. 'But I haven't had anything.'

'Oh yes you have,' said Errol. 'You've been standing there beside my van for ages and you've had the lovely smell of my fish and chips free. Your bread wouldn't have tasted half as nice without it.'

Jock was astonished. He turned to a well-dressed man who was starting to eat some fish and chips next to him.

'Have you ever heard anything as mean as that?' asked Jock.

'Oh he's quite right, you know,' said the man, who happened to be old and wise and was once a judge. 'Such a lovely smell must be paid for.'

Jock looked even more worried and astonished.

'How much have you got?' asked the judge. From the bottom of his pocket Jock pulled out all the money he had – one lonely 5p piece.

'May I?' said the judge. He took the 5p and walked over to Errol with it.

'Hold that for a minute,' he said to the van owner.

Errol grinned with triumph. The old man knew what he was on about. Errol was going to make a little bit more money – and this time for nothing. But no sooner had he got the coin in his hand than the judge took it away again.

'But . . .' began Errol.

'There we are, fair payment,' said the judge. 'He has paid you for the *smell* of your fish and chips with the *feel* of his money.'

Prayer
How much better it would have been if Errol had had kind thoughts instead of mean and selfish ones. Then perhaps he might have *given* Jock something to eat. Let us pray that we will choose to do kind acts instead of mean and selfish ones.

Hymn
'The wise may bring their learning' (*Come and Praise* No 64)

Information for the teacher
Many folk tales contain a similar 'message' to this story, with a mean person being shown up by the wit or wisdom of another. For similar tales see the Turkish stories of Nasr-ud-Din; Anansi tales, or Brer Rabbit.

A new start   *People*

Introduction
Imagine what it would be like if you went out of school – and you couldn't find your Mum, or your Dad, or your house, or anybody you knew. Wouldn't it be dreadful!

This morning's story took place in a country called Vietnam. Once there was a terrible war there, and lots of children lost their homes and everybody they knew. This is the story of one of them.

Story
Two ladies walked down a village street in Vietnam. They were nuns (that means they spent their whole lives helping other people and praying to God). There had been a terrible battle. All around there were broken-down lorries and burnt-out cars. There was a smell of smoke everywhere.

'Listen,' said one of the nuns. 'I thought I heard something.'

'Yes, it came from behind that car,' said the other.

They walked over and looked behind the wreckcd car. A small girl of about three was sitting there and playing with an old steering wheel. When she saw the nuns she gave them a big smile.

'Isn't she lovely,' said one of the nuns. 'Let's call her 'Happiness'.'

The nuns could not find anybody who knew anything about the little girl. They guessed that all her family had been killed in the war. So they took Happiness with them to the nearest town, which was called Saigon.

'There is only one thing for it,' said one of the nuns. 'We'll have to get in touch with those people in England who have said they will adopt orphans from Vietnam.'

So the nuns wrote a letter to a family in England, called Merryweather.

'Marvellous news!' gasped Mrs Merryweather when she read the letter. Mr Merryweather and the three Merryweather girls asked her to explain.

'That's wonderful,' said Mr Merryweather. 'Now we'll be able to give a home to someone who has not been as lucky as our three children here.'

And so little Happiness was put on an aeroplane in Vietnam and flown to England. Mrs Merryweather met her and she soon became one of the family. She still had the lovely smile which caused the nuns to call her 'Happiness', but now she was called Maria Merryweather.

Prayer
Let us pray this morning for an end to all wars and fighting. Let us pray for those people who, even as we think about these things, have been hurt or made homeless by wars somewhere in the world. Let us think of children who have lost their families, and let us hope that in the future the world will be a more peaceful place.

Hymn
'Thank you, Lord' (*Come and Praise* No 32)

Information for the teacher
1   Reference to the Bible indicates that wars mentioned there were instigated for the same reasons as now – to make territorial gains; to increase resources; to establish new ideologies. The Old Testament denounces killing (Exodus 20:13) and praises the benefits of peace (Lev 26:6; Kings 2, 31–33). 'All who take the sword will perish by the sword' (Matthew 26:52).

2   When Happiness became Maria Merryweather she was making a new beginning. 'Beginnings' could be discussed in the context of children beginning the school day with an assembly; with Muslims saying a prayer at dawn; with Hindus saying a prayer as their foot touches the ground for the first time on a new day.

3   Useful addresses for further work on children finding new homes could
    be:
    Church of England Children's Society, Old Town Hall, Kennington Road,
    London SE11 4QD.
    Dr Barnado's Homes, Tanners Lane, Barkingside, Ilford, Essex.

Janet thinks quickly   *People*

Introduction

'Go away – you are too young to help.' Has anybody ever said that to you?
Or perhaps they have said, 'Go away, you are too small to help.'

This morning's story is about somebody who was very young and very
small, but she still managed to help out.

Story

Janet was five years old. She had three big brothers who were older than her.

'Leave that Janet, I'll do it for you.'

'You're too small to lift that, Janet, let me do it.'

'Keep out of my way Janet.'

These were the sort of things Janet's brothers were always saying to her.
Then one day Janet's mother had to go into hospital. Before she went, she
got Janet and her brothers together.

'Now, while I'm away,' she said, 'I want you to behave yourselves and
don't be a nuisance to your dad. And you three, make sure you look after
Janet.'

'OK Mum,' replied Paul, Jim and Richard.

Mum went off to hospital and that night Dad said to the children, 'As
soon as we've had our tea we're going to the hospital to see Mum.'

Soon they were all ready to go. Dad opened the garage door and began
to back the car out. The children waited on the steep drive which dropped
down to a very busy road. When the car was halfway out of the garage it
stopped.

'I've forgotten those grapes,' said Dad as he jumped out. 'Won't be a
minute.'

He went back into the house. Then suddenly, Janet pointed: 'Look, Look!'
she cried. 'The car.'

Dad had forgotten to put the brake on. The car was starting to roll down
the drive!

'Quick,' yelled Paul to his brothers, and they dashed to the back of the car and threw all their weight against it. For a moment the car held, but the drive was too steep and the car so heavy that it soon began to move slowly downwards again. The boys' feet slipped as they desperately tried to hold it.

Then Janet remembered the small pieces of wood Dad called 'chocks'. Running into the garage she grabbed two of them from the shelf where they were kept. She raced back outside and pushed a chock under one of the slowly moving back wheels, and then hurried round to do the same on the other side. Racing back to the garage she found two more and did the same to the front wheels.

'It's holding!' yelled Paul. Leaping away from the back of the car he opened the driver's door and yanked on the brake.

Just at that moment Dad came back out of the house.

'What's been going on?' he asked.

'Quite a lot!' said Paul. 'Janet has been terrific. Without her quick thinking there would have been a nasty accident.'

Prayer

This morning, let us remember that no matter how young or small we might be, we might be suddenly called upon to think and act quickly in an emergency. Let us pray that if this happens, like Janet, we will take the right action.

Hymn

'One more step' (*Come and Praise* No 47)

Information for the teacher

1 A story such as this could naturally provoke more discussion on safety in various places. A useful address in this context is:
   Royal Society for the Prevention of Accidents, Cannon House, The Priory, Queensway, Birmingham B4 6BS

2 Stories like this one appear in newspapers from time to time. They could be collected into a scrapbook. This would be interesting for the children to look at − and in the long term it can form a valuable assembly resource for the teacher.

What really counts   *Qualities*

Introduction

If you had a magic wish − what would you wish for? Would you like to have a BMX or a pony; a video or a computer?

When you have heard today's story it might make you think again about what you would wish for. The story is about two men who lived long ago in Africa. They both wished for money – and their wish came true. Listen to what happened next.

Story

Kwadjo looked at the small pile of gold in front of him.

'That's great,' he said, rubbing his hands. 'With this gold I can buy animals, feed them up and then sell them for more gold. Soon I'll have more gold than anybody else around!'

So Kwadjo set about using his gold to make him more gold. He spent all his days buying and selling. He hadn't time to make any friends and, to tell you the truth, nobody liked him much, because all he was interested in was getting the best price he could.

'Aha,' he said to himself. 'I must be the richest man around. I've got even more than that fellow Ago.'

Now Ago was the other man whose wish for money had come true. As he looked at his pile of gold he too thought to himself, 'With this money I'll be able to buy some really beautiful clothes.'

So Ago bought long, richly-coloured robes which were the most beautiful anybody had ever seen.

'There's no doubt,' said Ago to himself. 'I am the best dressed man in this village and the next. I'm not going to talk to anybody unless they are dressed as beautifully as I am.'

Well, he couldn't find anybody who was dressed as well as he was – so soon as he wasn't talking to a single person. Things got so bad that he started talking to himself!

'This is no good,' he said. 'I'm the best dressed man around – and yet I am unhappy. I must go and see Anna, the wise old woman of the village.'

Well, as Ago was going towards Anna's house, who should he see in front of him but Kwadjo.

'That's Kwadjo,' said Ago to himself. 'Everybody knows he's the richest man in these parts. What on earth can he be going to see Anna about?'

When Ago got to Anna's she asked him to come in. Soon both he and Kwadjo were pouring out their troubles to Anna. They were so lonely, and it was so long since they'd talked to anybody properly that they could hardly stop!

Finally Anna interrupted.

'My friends', she said. 'You have both learned your lesson before you came here. Bags of gold and fine clothes won't make you happy because you can't talk to either of them. Try spending your money to help others and then you will find something more precious than either gold or clothes – friends.'

Prayer

Let us spend a few seconds thinking quietly about the good things in our lives. In the quietness, let us think about the children round us, our friends. Let us remember how very important friends are. Let us pray that each of us has the qualities to be a good friend.

Hymn

'The wise may bring their learning' (*Come and Praise* No 64)

Information for the teacher

1   It is possible to take this story a stage further, eg: Kwadjo and Ago learn that the pursuit of material gain brings no happiness – but sharing this wealth would help others. The *Declaration of Human Rights* issued by the United Nations in 1948 said that everyone should have a standard of living which would ensure the well-being of themselves and their dependants. This can only be achieved by 'aid' from those who are better off.

2   The parable of the Good Samaritan (Luke 10: 25-37) can be used here and in many other contexts. In connection with this story the preliminaries to the parable might be particularly useful as when the lawyer asks Jesus: 'And who is my neighbour?' (friend)

3   Luke 11: 5–11, provides another reading about friendship which, when put into appropriate language is suitable for virtually any age group.

The visitor   *Qualities*

Introduction

This morning's story is about something that took place in a small village a very long time ago. In this village lived a rich man and a poor tailor. One day a beggar came along – and strange things happened.

Story

Mr and Mrs Plenty were very rich. They lived in a big house and Mrs Plenty was always telling anybody who would listen how important her husband was.

One day Mrs Plenty was making a meal for herself and her husband. She had chicken and potatoes, carrots, peas and cauliflower. There was lots of gravy to put on the chicken. For sweet she had a huge strawberry cream cake. She was just about to lay the table for this meal when there was a knock on the door.

'Who can that be?' thought Mrs Plenty, irritably.

When she opened the door she saw a poor, thin man standing there. His face was pale with cold and his clothes were in tatters.

'I'm sorry to bother you,' he said, 'but I wonder if you could spare me a little food . . . I haven't had anything to eat for such a long time.'

Mrs Plenty took a deep breath.

'How dare you come knocking on my door. My husband and I are just about to sit down and eat and we don't like to be disturbed. Now, be off with you!'

Then she slammed the door in the beggar's face.

Meanwhile, just down the road, Mrs Kindly the tailor's wife was cooking too. She had a chicken as well, but it had to feed the whole family. Mr and Mrs Kindly had six children so there was hardly enough food to go round. They couldn't afford to have any pudding at all. Just as Mrs Kindly was serving the meal there was a knock on the door. Mrs Kindly answered it.

'Oh you poor man,' she said, when she saw the pale, thin beggar there.

'I'm sorry to bother you,' he said, 'but I wondered if you could spare me a little . . . '

'Come in,' said Mrs Kindly. 'Come in at once.'

When the beggar got inside, Mrs Kindly found a chair for him. Soon the six children and the the three grown-ups were enjoying their chicken. When the beggar finished he pushed his chair back.

'That was wonderful,' he said. 'Thank you very, very much. Now I'll get on my way.'

'Nonsense, nonsense,' replied Mr Kindly. 'It's much too late and too cold to go out there. You must stay the night and have a good rest. My wife and I will sleep on the carpet and you take our bed.'

'Oh I couldn't do that . . . ' began the beggar, but Mr Kindly insisted.

The beggar had a lovely comfortable night's sleep and next morning he got up and prepared to go.

'You have been very kind,' he said to the tailor. 'If I could give you anything you wished for, what would you choose?'

'Oh, we've only done what anybody else would have done,' smiled the tailor. 'We certainly don't want anything.'

So the beggar went on his way. But not long after that, a very strange thing happened. No matter how much material Mr Kindly cut off his bales of cloth to make clothes – there was still some left! He never, ever, had to buy any more cloth.

Soon Mr Kindly and his family were not only happy but quite well off too. Now they could have two chickens for their meal – and a pudding too. But when Mr and Mrs Plenty heard the story they were filled with jealousy.

Prayer

Let us pray that we can be kind people who will always do a good turn for others without expecting a reward.

Hymn

'Lord of all hopefulness' (*Come and Praise* No 52)

Information for the teacher

1   There is an old Japanese saying:
    'The beggar was given a horse but he would rather have had a meal.'
    This, along with the assembly story, could be used to discuss the importance of the right kind of 'giving'.

2   Taking this theme of giving appropriately a stage further, reference could be made to the following words of Confucius:
    'Give a man a fish and you feed him for a day,
    Teach a man to fish and you feed him for life.'
    Some excellent material to back up this philosophy is contained in the 1986 Christian Aid pamphlet *Good news for a change – suggestions for use with children under 11.* This material can be obtained free from:
    Christian Aid, PO Box No 1, London SW9 8BH

The parachute   *Qualities*

Introduction

I expect all of you have seen pictures on TV of people making parachute jumps. You will have noticed how the parachute slows them down as they fall through the air, so that they land on the ground safely.

This morning's story is about two soldiers. Both of them jumped from an aeroplane to make a parachute jump, but this time . . . something went wrong!

Story

Bill was very excited.

'This is going to be great,' he said. 'My first parachute jump – I can hardly wait!'

Bill was training to be a special kind of soldier called a paratrooper. As part of his training he had to make a parachute jump from an aeroplane. Today was the day of his first jump.

'Come on, come on, hurry up there,' shouted the sergeant in charge of the soldiers, whose name was Terry. Bill and the other soldiers crowded into the aeroplane. Then it roared down the runway and swept into the sky. Higher and higher it climbed.

'Now,' said Terry. 'I'm going to jump out first. Watch me – and then follow.'

The door of the aeroplane was open. For a moment, Terry stood in the howling wind. Then he threw himself into the sky.

As soon as Terry had gone, Bill, who was next in line, jumped out of the aeroplane. The first thing he noticed was the quietness after the roar of the plane. He felt himself falling quickly, but he could still enjoy the marvellous views.

'Well, better get my parachute open now,' thought Bill, and he pulled the handle to open it. He waited for the 'crack' as the white, umbrella-like parachute opened above him. But it never came – and Bill began to fall faster and faster.

'My parachute – there's something wrong!' gasped Bill. 'I'm going to be killed!'

Desperately he tried everything he knew to get the parachute open. It was no good, it just would not budge. By now the ground was rushing towards him and Bill was terrified.

Meanwhile, lower down, Terry had heard Bill's shouts. Looking up he saw the young soldier falling quickly through the air while he struggled with his parachute. Within seconds Bill was passing him but as he did so, Terry reached out and grabbed the young soldier. Immediately Terry began to fall much faster, too, because his parachute now had double weight to carry.

'Hang on, soldier,' Terry called to Bill. 'Wrap your legs round me as well as your arms.'

The two men were coming down to land much quicker than they should have done.

'Keep a tight grip', shouted Terry. 'I'm going to try to steer us towards that long, soggy grass over there.'

Swinging wildly the two men clung to each other as the parachute swept them over some marshy land. The ground came up to meet them with frightening speed and then – crash!

'Are you all right?' asked Bill as he pulled himself out of the grass, weeds and mud.

'I think I'm going to need a bit of help,' muttered Terry.

It was later found that Terry had broken both of his legs, but by his courage and quick-thinking he had certainly saved Bill's life.

Prayer

Let us think this morning about those people who are so brave that they risk their lives to help others. Let us give thanks for the bravery we hear about in stories like this.

Hymn
'Let us with a gladsome mind' (*Come and Praise* No 8)

Information for the teacher
1   This story is adapted from a true incident involving two members of the Parachute Regiment. The accident was made worse by the fact that the one remaining parachute had begun to collapse when the paratroopers were still 700 feet from the ground. But for soft ground and long grass it is likely that both men would have been killed.

2   A useful address in connection with this story is:
The British Parachute Association, 75 Victoria Street, London SW1

One good turn deserves another   *Qualities*

Introduction
Perhaps you have heard your teacher, or your Mum, say: 'One good turn deserves another.' This morning's story is about one good turn – and then another. It starts with an old cobbler who lived with his wife in a tiny cottage.

Story
'Oh dear, oh dear, oh dear,' said Johann.

'What is it?' asked Monika, his wife.

'I've only got enough leather left to make one pair of shoes. How are we going to live?'

'We'll manage somehow,' said Monika. 'Look, cut the leather ready to make the shoes and then come to bed. You'll feel much more cheerful after a good night's sleep.'

Next morning Johann woke early. He got straight out of bed because he wanted to get the shoes made. No sooner had he rubbed the sleep from his eyes than he looked at the table – and gasped! Instead of pieces of leather lying on it – there was a beautifully made pair of shoes!

'But I didn't make them,' thought Johann, 'and I don't think I got up and made them in my sleep. Perhaps I'm dreaming.'

To make sure he wasn't he woke Monika up. At first she was rather annoyed to be woken up so early but when she saw the shoes she said, 'They're no dream'.

That day Johann sold the shoes. They were so well made that the customer who bought them gave Johann enough money to buy the leather to make two more pairs.

That night Johann cut the leather into strips again so that he could start work early in the morning. Then he and Monika went to bed.

Early next morning Johann slowly opened one eye and looked at the table. He could not believe it! There, on the table, were *two* beautifully-made pairs of shoes!

That day he sold the two pairs of shoes and then got enough leather to make four pairs. That night he left out the leather and, sure enough, there were four, newly-made pairs of shoes waiting for him next morning.

'It's marvellous,' said Monika, 'but we must stay up to see who is making these shoes so that we can thank them properly.'

That night Johann and Monika lay in their bed pretending to be asleep, but really they were not. At midnight they heard a shuffling noise and, peeping over the bedclothes, they saw two little elves come in and go straight to the table. For an hour the two little men worked silently and quickly and, sure enough, eight pairs of beautifully-made shoes lay on the table when they had finished. When their work was done they vanished.

'Amazing,' said Johann, 'but, the poor little fellows had no clothes.'

'Yes,' replied Monika. 'Now I know we can do *them* a good turn.'

That day Johann again sold the shoes quickly and then he got to work and made two tiny pairs of boots. Monika worked all day sewing tiny shirts, trousers and jackets. When they had finished, instead of leaving leather on the table, Monika and Johann left the tiny boots and clothes. Then they went to bed and pretended to be asleep again.

Sure enough, at midnight, the two little men suddenly appeared. At first they seemed surprised that there was no leather on the table, then they noticed the clothes and boots. Even though they were only watching by firelight Monika and Johann could see the delight in the little men's eyes as they realised the clothes and boots were for them. They dressed quickly, then they stood and admired each other, slapped each other on the back – and disappeared.

From that day on they never came back, but now Johann was the most famous shoemaker in the district and he was never poor again. As for the little men, well, perhaps they are doing somebody else a good turn now.

Prayer

Let us think this morning of giving help wherever and whenever we can. Let us always try to be helpful at home and at school.

Hymn
'The best gift' (*Come and Praise* No 59)

Information for the teacher
This story is an adaptation of one by the Brothers Grimm. An excellent selection of folk tales from a wide variety of countries is *My First Big Story Book* by Richard Bamberger (Puffin, 1969).

Who is best?   *Qualities*

Introduction
None of us like people who boast and brag and tell us how good they are. This morning's story is about three shopkeepers who all sold sweets in the same town. You'll see what I mean about boasting if you listen carefully!

Story
Newtown was just what its name suggests. It was a new town. Lots of people moved into new houses there and a great big shopping precinct was opened in the centre of town. Every day more and more people came to look at the shops and buy things. Now it so happened that there were three sweet shops all in one street.

Bob and Mary owned the first sweet shop.

'We've got to get more people to buy their sweets here,' said Bob to Mary. 'How are we gong to do that?'

'Hmm,' replied Mary. 'We'll, we've got to say that we are the best sweet shop. Let's put a notice in the window.'

The next day a huge notice appeared in Bob's sweet shop window. It said: *Buy your sweets here – the best sweet shop in town!*

Bob and Mary smiled when they looked at the notice. They were very pleased with themselves.

Later that day the owners of the second sweet shop saw the sign.

'Look at that,' said Elvira to Mitch. 'We'll have to put up a notice to get people to come to our shop instead of this one.'

'You're absolutely right,' replied Mitch, and the next day he put up a notice. It said: *Buy your sweets here – this is the world's best sweet shop!*

Elvira and Mitch were pleased.

That's a better notice than their's,' said Elvira smugly.

Later the same day Petronella and Errol, who owned the third sweet shop, walked along the street. They looked at the notice in Bob's shop but they also noticed that the floor in his shop was rather dirty and Mary's overall could have been cleaner.

Petronella and Errol then looked in Mitch's shop. They read the notice but then they noticed that the sweets were arranged in a higgledy-piggledy way and everything looked rather untidy.

'Well,' said Petronella, 'I think we should put a notice up too, and I know what we should say.'

'I agree my dear,' replied Errol. A few minutes later a neat notice went up in the window of his neat, clean and beautifully arranged shop. It said: *Buy your sweets here – at the best sweet shop in this street.*

Can you guess where most people went to buy their sweets?

(adapted from an old French tale)

Prayer
Let us think about being honest. Let us not be boastful, and always be ready to admit our faults. Let us behave in a way which makes us a person other people know they can trust.

Hymn
'The wise may bring their learning' (*Come and Praise* No 64)

Information for the teacher
1   As might be expected, both the Old and the New Testament abound in references which uphold the value of truth and condemn any form of falsifying: Exodus 20:16; Proverbs 12: 17–22; Ephesians 4: 15; John 2:21; Revelations 22:15.

2   If we assume that boastfulness in this story is motivated by greed then two useful references might be:
'Money gets respect, fame and wisdom – that this should be the case is a shame.' (Hindu saying)
'The poor man finds it hard not to complain, the rich man finds it hard not to boast.' (adapted from a saying by Confucius)

The man who helped everybody   *Qualities*

Introduction
There was once a great battle taking place. The soldiers on one side were

called Sikhs, and the soldiers on the other side were called Muslims. During a pause in the battle a soldier brought a prisoner to the tent of the Sikh leader, Gobind Singh.

Story

'Get in there,' shouted the soldier. The doors of the tent were opened and the prisoner was pushed inside. Gobind Singh, the leader of the Sikhs, looked up.

'Why have you brought this man to me?' he asked.

'Sir, he is a traitor to our side,' said the soldier.

'Oh, how is that?' asked Gobind Singh.

'Well,' went on the soldier, 'he has been giving things to our enemies and helping them.'

'Well sir,' said the man, whose name was Ghanava, 'it's like this. My job is to carry water round the battlefield. When I see anybody who is wounded I stop and give him a drink to try and ease the pain.'

'Go on,' said Gobind Singh.

'He's been giving the wounded *enemy* soldiers drinks sir,' interrupted the soldier.

'Is that true?' asked Gobind Singh.

'Yes,' answered Ghanava. 'When I look down and see somebody who is badly wounded or even dying I don't see a Muslim or a Sikh, I just see a man who is hurt and needs help.'

There was a pause and then Gobind Singh spoke again.

'You are a good man, Ghanava,' he said. 'From now on not only can you give water to anybody who is wounded, but I will give you some ointment so that you can help to heal their wounds as well.'

And so Ghanava continued to help anybody who was hurt – no matter which side that person was on.

Prayer

This morning let us listen to some words which Gobind Singh himself wrote:

'All men are the same even though they look different,

The light and the dark, the ugly and the beautiful.

All human beings have the same eyes and the same ears.'

Hymn

'A man for all the people' (*Come and Praise* No 27)

Information for the teacher

1   After this incident Ghanava became famous. He was given the name Bhai Ghanava. *Bhai* is a word which means brother, and it is given only to people of very special qualities.

2   This story could also be used in a special occasion theme linked to the Sikh celebration of Gobind Singh's birthday. Because of the variables of Indian calendars it is impossible to be precise about exactly when this is commemorated each year, but the assembly could be used in the month of January.

3   This story could also be linked with that of Henri Dunant, founder of the Red Cross, another organisation which seeks to give aid no matter which side victims are on.

Doctor to the rescue   *Qualities*

Introduction

This morning's story is about a doctor. It took place in London, not very long ago.

One morning a lady went to light the gas in her flat and there was a terrible explosion. The whole block of flats came crashing down and lots of people were trapped in the wreckage. Eve was one of these people. She was badly hurt and desperately needed a doctor.

Story

Eve didn't know where she hurt most. She had been in the kitchen of her flat when there was a terrible bang. The next thing she knew was that the roof was falling on top of her, she was trapped.

'If only I could move all these bricks and wood I might be able to crawl out,' she said to herself. But try as she might she couldn't move the pile of wreckage which trapped her leg. She also knew from the pain that her leg was broken.

'It's no good, I'll just have to wait until somebody can get me out,' Eve thought. Then she looked at all the bricks and broken furniture piled around about, and on top of her, and wondered if anybody would ever find her.

'I know,' she thought, 'every minute or so I'll shout for help.' Taking a deep breath she shouted out as loud as she could: 'Help!'

Meanwhile, outside the wreckage of the flats, policemen, firemen, doctors and nurses were trying to find and rescue injured people. Every few minutes they stopped what they were doing and kept absolutely still and silent – so that they could hear anybody who might be calling for help.

Among the rescuers was a very, very big man. His name was Doctor Barry Powell. When everything was quiet he heard a faint cry of 'Help!'

'Listen,' he said to some firemen near him, 'it's coming from under that enormous pile of wreckage. I must crawl in there and see if I can help.'

'No, no,' said the firemen. 'It's too dangerous. Any minute now that's all going to come crashing down!'

'Never mind that – we must help that poor woman who is trapped.'

'Well it's better if one of us goes,' said the firemen.

'No it isn't,' replied Doctor Powell. 'The woman may be injured and as I am a doctor I should be able to help when I reach her.'

So the doctor started to crawl along the tiny passage through the wreckage. It was only 18 inches wide; every time he moved, the bricks tore his shirt and trousers and scraped the skin off his knees and elbows. Inch by inch he crawled towards the voice which called 'Help' every minute or so.

After what seemed a very long time Barry reached Eve. He could see at once that she was badly hurt.

'Hello,' said Eve, when she saw him. She smiled bravely, 'I'm glad you've come.'

'Don't worry,' said Barry, 'we'll soon have you out, but I must get something to help you because you are hurt.'

So Barry crawled out of the tiny passage and then came back with some medicine and equipment to help Eve. As he did so the wreckage creaked and groaned as if it would fall any minute.

Barry gave Eve something to ease the pain in her leg. Then he shouted to the firemen to come in, and, clearing a bigger passage, they carefully dragged Eve to safety. Once outside the wrecked flats she was rushed to hospital.

But for Barry's skill and bravery Eve would probably have died. Afterwards, Barry was much more ready to talk about Eve than himself. 'She's a very, very brave lady,' he said. 'She never panicked and did all she could to help, even though she was in great pain.'

Prayer
Let us say a special prayer for doctors and nurses all over the world. Let us give thanks for their courage and the way they care for us when we are ill or injured.

Hymn
'Somebody greater' (*Come and Praise* No 5)

Information for the teacher
The background to this story was a gas explosion in Putney Hill, West London in January 1985. The explosion wrecked a block of flats and killed eight people. Miss Eve Krejci was saved by the courage and detemination of

Doctor Barry Powell of Queen Mary's Hospital, Roehampton. Dr Powell's action was all the more remarkable because at 17 stone he was obviously at a disadvantage when trying to crawl through narrow openings in the rubble.

Miss Krejci was trapped for almost seven hours and Dr Powell described her as being 'extraordinarily brave.'

Saint Elisabeth
Qualities

Introduction
When we call a person a saint we usually mean that they have done something very special to help other people. Today's story took place a long time ago. In a far off country a cruel king called Ludwig made life miserable for his people. Although the king was a cruel and hated man, his wife was very different. This is her story.

Story
Elisabeth was sad and worried.

'What am I to do?' she wondered. 'These people *must* have food.'

The people she was talking about were ruled by her husband King Ludwig. Ludwig treated his subjects very badly indeed. They were so poor that many were starving. When Elisabeth found out about this she began to make journeys out of the castle to give bread to these unfortunate people. But this made Ludwig very angry.

'It must stop at once!' he thundered. 'These people must learn to fend for themselves. You will give them neither food nor money!'

'But . . . ' began Elisabeth.

'There is nothing for you to say,' went on Ludwig, 'and to make sure you do as you are told you are forbidden to leave the castle.'

So Elisabeth was a prisoner in her own home. This did not worry her as much as what was happening to the people outside. One day she could stand it no longer. While Ludwig was out hunting she went to the castle kitchens. There she collected as much bread as she could, crammed it into a basket and put a cloth over it. Then she left the castle and hurried towards the village.

As bad luck would have it, that was the very moment that Ludwig was returning from his hunting trip. Seeing Elisabeth on the pathway he was furious that she had disobeyed his orders, and even more furious at the thought of what was in the basket and where she was taking it.

'Stop!' he ordered.

The horsemen around him reined to a halt. Elisabeth stopped, pale and frightened.

'What is in that basket?' snapped Ludwig.

Elisabeth knew that Ludwig might even put her to death for disobeying his orders. Suddenly, without thinking about it, she blurted out,

'The basket is full of roses.'

Angrily Ludwig bent down and hurled the cloth off the basket. It was full of deep red roses.

Prayer
'Let us give thanks for those who make life better and more purposeful for everybody.'

(adapted from a Parsee prayer)

Hymn
'The King of Love' (*Come and Praise* No 54)

Information for the teacher
1   St Elisabeth of Hungary lived in the thirteenth century. She was the daughter of King Andreas of Hungary. She was betrothed to Ludwig as an infant, and taken to live with his family, where she was lonely and badly-treated. In Christian art she is usually protrayed with an apron full of roses. There are many legends about her, all telling of her kindness and concern for others.

2   For more details on saints a useful book is *Festivals and Saints' Days* by V J Green (Blandford Press, 1978).

3   Roses have been symbolic flowers for several cultures. To the ancient Romans the rose symbolised victory and love (it was the flower of Venus, goddess of love).

    For Christians the red rose has symbolised martyrdom and the white rose purity. According to one legend, in Paradise the rose grew without thorns – it acquired them to remind man of his sins.

The gift   *Qualities*

Introduction
A long time ago, in a hot land far from England there lived a good and wise man. He was called Lord Buddha.

Story

Lord Buddha was sitting underneath a tree. He was there for a special reason.

'Let it be known to everybody,' he said, 'that I am going to sit under this tree and collect gifts for poor people who are desperately in need.'

The news spread quickly and soon people began to arrive beside the Buddha's tree. The first person was a rich and powerful king.

'My Lord,' he said to Lord Buddha, 'I cannot carry my gift, but you can have the house I own just over the hill, and all the land that goes with it.'

'Thank you,' said the Buddha.

'I have brought all these jewels,' said a prince, who was next in line. One of his servants then put a huge box of jewels on the ground beside the Buddha.

'Thank you,' said Lord Buddha.

'I have brought this gold,' said a wealthy merchant who was next, 'and my friend here has brought an equal amount of silver.'

'Thank you,' said Lord Buddha.

So the morning went on. One generous person after another gave gold or silver or jewels or land. Most had their servants with them to carry things and all stayed to talk to each other after making their gifts. It was late in the morning when they noticed somebody, not like themselves, who had joined the line of givers.

'What on earth has she got to give?' asked one rich man.

'Ridiculous – she can't have anything of value,' said a prince.

'I don't suppose Lord Buddha will be much interested in her,' muttered a rich landowner.

The person they were talking about was an old woman. Unlike all the well dressed princes and merchants she had on only old rags. She carried nothing to protect her from the hot sun and in her hands she carried only a pomegranate.

Eventually she reached the Buddha. He had not moved all morning, sitting still and only saying thank you to all the givers. The old woman spoke.

'Forgive me, Lord Buddha, for I have very little to offer. This pomegranate is my food for today, but when I heard you were collecting for the poor I thought there would surely be somebody even worse off than me – so I have brought you the pomengranate.'

'My dear lady, how kind of you,' said Lord Buddha. He stood up, leaving the shade of his tree, and walked towards the poor woman to take the pomegranate from her. 'Thank you very, very much.'

The people watching mumbled amongst themselves.

'I gave him a house and all he said was 'thank you'.'

'He didn't make a fuss of me like that – and I gave him gold!'

'He didn't even get up when I gave him some jewels.'

The Buddha heard all these comments and he spoke.

'Those of you who are well off, gave me something of what you had. This poor woman gave me everything she had.'

Prayer

Our prayer this morning is one which Lord Buddha himself might have said. 'The people who are best off are those who are kind to others and think only kind thoughts.'

(This is a free adaptation of a Buddhist saying: 'The greatest wealth consists of being charitable; the greatest happiness is having tranquility of mind)

Hymn

'The best gift' (*Come and Praise* No 59)

Information for the teacher

1 Siddhartha Gautama was a rich Indian prince, born about 560 years before Christ. After his rich and protected upbringing he was so horrified to see the suffering in the world that he became a beggar. He ultimately realised that the middle way, between seeking luxurious living and enduring torment, is the best path to happiness and enlightenment. Siddhartha earned the title *Buddha* which means 'the enlightened one'.

2 There are some Buddhists in Great Britain but the majority are in Sri Lanka, Tibet, SE Asia, Japan and China. Peace, kindness and self-denial are the traditional virtues of the religion.

3 It is interesting that the featured fruit (pomegranate) in this story was also a popular and highly symbolic one to the Jews. Pomegranates grow near Cana of Galilee and were regarded as symbols of rain and fertility. The large numbers of seeds symbolised the birth of many children. Drawings of pomegranates appeared on early coins of the area.

4 A useful address for more information is:
Buddhist Society, 58 Eccleston Square, London SW1V 1PH.

The princess with seven brothers   *Qualities*

Introduction

One of the best qualities to have is honesty. People will always trust a person who is honest. On the other hand, if we deliberately tell lies and try to deceive other people – then trouble lies ahead! You will see what I mean when you listen to this morning's story.

Story

Ute was a princess. She lived with her mother, the queen, and her father, the king. Although they were kind to her, Ute was rather unhappy. There was a reason for this.

'Mother,' she said. 'You are always telling me about the seven brothers I have, but I never see them.'

'Of course not, my dear,' replied the queen. 'They live many miles away from here.'

'But I cannot remember them at all,' said Ute. 'Can I go and visit them?'

'Well, you can,' said the queen, 'but it is far too long and dangerous a ride for you to go by yourself. You will have to take one of the servants with you.'

So it was arranged and Ute, along with a servant girl of her own age called Monika, set out on the journey. As they rode along, Ute told Monika how she couldn't remember what her brothers looked like – and how she was sure they wouldn't know her.

Finally they almost reached the place where the brothers lived.

'Let's stop here a minute by this stream,' said Ute. 'I am going to wash my face and have a drink.'

So saying she got down from the horse.

No sooner had she done this than Monika seized the reins of Ute's horse, lashed her own with a whip, and galloped off. Within a few hours she arrived at the town where the brothers lived and found their castle. She told them that she was Ute, their sister, who had grown up whilst they were away. The brothers were absolutely delighted. They made a great fuss of Monika, giving her everything they had. Two days later a tired, dirty and unhappy Ute turned up at the castle.

'I'm your sister,' she said to the first brother she met.

'Nonsense,' he replied. 'Our sister is already with us. We could do with another servant though – would you like to stay to look after the hens?'

So Ute became a servant for her brothers. Monika, worried that the truth would come out, treated Ute very badly in the hope that she would go away. The brothers noticed this.

'Could a sister of ours really behave so badly?' one of them asked.

'What's more, the servant girl never complains,' said another.

'Well, I didn't ever tell you,' said the third, 'but the servant girl claims she is our sister.'

'What!'

'Now you come to mention it, our sister came here with two horses. Why should she need two?'

'Unless . . . '

So the brothers got Ute and Monika together. Soon it was obvious who was telling the truth. Bursting into tears, Monika confessed everything. She was sent away in disgrace and the brothers were delighted to have found their real sister.

(adapted from an Albanian folk tale)

Prayer
This morning we will think again about the story we have just heard, and about being honest. Let us remember the words of a Jewish prayer: 'The world is made a better place by three things – justice, peace, and truth.'

Hymn
'I listen and I listen' (*Come and Praise* No 60)

Information for the teacher
There are many volumes of folk tales from which stories with suitable 'moral' points can be extracted and used for assembly. A useful and inexpensive series, written in language ideal for infants, is *My First (Second/Third) Big Story Book*, compiled by Richard Bamberger and published by Young Puffin.

The teddy bear story   *Qualities*

Introduction
(It would be very useful if a teddy bear, or a picture of one, was shown in conjunction with this introduction.) I think all of us have had teddy bears at some time. Thousands of children must have gone to bed with teddy bears! This morning's story is about how teddy bears came to be.

Story
One of the things none of us can choose is the name our parents give us when we are born. As we grow older, some of us like our names and some of us don't. Some people dislike their names so much that they change them.

'I hate my name,' said a young boy one day. 'I'm going to make sure nobody calls me by it.'

This boy's name was Theodore, but whenever anybody asked him what he was called he alway said 'Teddy'.

Well, when Teddy grew up he became a very famous man – he was President of the United States of America.

One day some men asked Teddy to go hunting with them.

'We'll shoot some bears,' they said.

Teddy wasn't too happy about this, but he went along. Some hours later he was lying behind a rock with his rifle ready.

'This is bear territory,' said his friends. 'Watch out.'

Teddy lay there, looking at the open ground in front of him. Then he saw a movement in the bushes. He held his breath. The bushes parted, and a bear came lumbering towards him.

But this wasn't a huge bear. It was small. It was a baby bear.

'I can't shoot that baby bear,' Teddy thought. 'How would a human being feel if someone shot their child. It would be terrible.'

So Teddy put his rifle on one side and kept very quiet. The baby bear trundled off to safety. When Teddy and his friends got back to town one of the friends told the story to a newspaper man. Next morning the story was in the papers and there was also a cartoon showing the baby bear and Teddy.

A man who made toys saw this cartoon.

'I've got an idea,' he thought. 'I'll make a cuddly toy which looks like a baby bear, and I'll call it 'Teddy Bear'. Everybody will remember this lovely story and they will want to buy the toy to remind them of it.'

The man who made toys then wrote to Teddy Roosevelt to ask if he could use his name in this way. Teddy said he would be pleased if he would. So the first Teddy Bears were made – and now you know how they got their name.

Prayer

Let us think this morning of very young children and very young animals. Let us remember how much care and looking after all babies need. Let us think particularly of people like doctors, nurses and vets who are there to give extra help and advice.

Hymn

'All creatures of our God and King' (*Come and Praise* No 7)

Information for the teacher

1   There is an International Teddy Bear Club (1 Dyers Buildings, Holborn, London EC1N 2JT). In the summer of 1985 it worked with Young Save the Children Fund (17 Grove Lane, Camberwell, London SE5 8RD) to raise money for Save the Children Fund.

2　Bears are mentioned in the Bible as enemies of the shepherd: 1 Samuel 17:34.

3　Bears feature often in children's stories. It would be possible to link this assembly to a Special Occasions/Christmas theme and incorporate the appropriate and sensitive reading about Paddington Bear's Christmas presents (and feelings) which can be found in *More about Paddington* by Michael Bond (Collins, 1959).

4　Theodore Roosevelt (1858–1919) was President of the USA from 1901–1909. For his efforts in aid of world peace he was awarded a Nobel Prize in 1906.

The shrinking chapatti　　　　　　　　　*Qualities*

Introduction

Do you know what a chapatti is? (Pause for answers.) So that we are all sure – it is a very thin piece of Indian bread. You make it with flour, margarine, salt and water. You mix these things together, then flatten them out and fry the flat shape on both sides.

This morning's story is about a chapatti.

Story

Niten and Shoaib were walking along one day. The sun was shining brightly overhead and they were hot, tired and very, very hungry.

'What's that lying on that stone over there?' said Niten suddenly.

'It's a . . . I don't believe it!' replied Shoaib. 'It's a lovely, tasty-looking chapatti.'

'I thought it was,' said Niten. 'It's a good job I saw it first – that means its mine.'

'Just a minute – you didn't even know what it was. I should have it,' claimed Shoaib.

'Now look here . . . ' started Niten angrily. Then a stranger appeared beside the two quarelling men.

'Excuse me,' he said. 'I couldn't help hearing your conversation and of course I can see the chapatti too. I am sure the best thing to do here would be for you to share the chapatti – and who better to divide it equally than me – after all I'm a stranger to you both.'

'Well it really should be mine . . . ' began Niten again.

'I tell you I should have it . . . ' continued Shoaib.

'Please my friends', said the stranger, and he went to the chapatti, picked it up and broke it into two pieces.

'Oh dear,' he said 'I seem to have made the two pieces uneven – I'll break another portion off the biggest piece.'

The stranger did this, put the portion he had taken off into his mouth, and ate it. Then he looked at the two pieces of chapatti he had left.

'Tut, tut, they are still uneven. We can't have that, I'll have to take a bit off this one now.' So saying he did the same thing again . . . and again . . . and again.

Finally, as Niten and Shoaib stared open-mouthed, the stranger said, 'Oh, I'm so sorry, these two pieces I have left are so small I wouldn't insult you by offering them.' He put the last of the chapatti in his mouth and hurried off down the road.

'But . . . ' began Niten.

'Exactly,' said Shoaib. 'We've been taught a lesson. If we hadn't argued and been greedy we could have shared that chapatti ourselves.'

(adapted from an Indian folk tale)

Prayer

> To want all
> is often
> to get nothing.
> To give freely
> is often
> to get more.

Hymn

'The journey of life' (*Come and Praise* No 45)

Information for the teacher

1   This story lends itself readily to simple and effective drama work. If a chapatti is not easily available a slice of bread would do just as well.

2   Greed – 'an inordinate desire to increase one's own share' – is illustrated in another way in the Bible story of the man who built bigger and better barns (Luke 12: 16–20).

3   The fact that so many people in India and other Third World countries are permanently hungry can be illustrated in a simple, symbolic way which young children can understand. Simplified statistics show that for every 5 people in Europe there are 12 slices of bread available; in India, for 11 people there are just 5 slices of bread available.

The sacks

Introduction

This morning's story took place a long, long time ago in a faraway country. It is about a king and a princess – and the two men who wanted to marry her.

The story tells how the king and the princess made their choice.

Story

There was a king who had a very beautiful daughter. The king's name was Rachid and his daughter was called Aliya. Now two young princes wanted to marry Aliya.

'Oh father,' said the princess, 'both Idriss and Mustapha want to marry me. I like them both. How can I choose?'

'Well my dear,' said King Rachid, 'the best thing to do is to give them a test. That will show us who is the best man.'

'What a good idea,' replied Princess Aliya. And so Idriss and Mustapha were called to the palace.

'As you both wish to marry my daughter,' said King Rachid, 'I am going to ask you to do something for us. This will help us to decide who will marry the princess.

Idriss, if you travel north for ten miles you will find a cave in the mountainside. Inside the cave you will find two sacks. Without looking to see what is in the sacks, leave one there to keep for yourself, and bring the other here to me.

Mustapha, you must travel south for ten miles. You will then find a cave containing two sacks also. You may keep one and bring the other to me.'

Idriss set off first. After riding hard he found the cave. Inside it was a soldier guarding two sacks. One of the sacks was big, one was small.

'Mmm,' thought Idriss. 'The king has got plenty of money. I might as well take him the small sack. If there's any treasure in them, that will leave me with the most. That's what I'll do.'

So he put the small sack on his horse and went back to the palace. He was nearly there when he saw Mustapha coming from the other direction. He had a very big sack on his horse's back.

'He's been stupid,' thought Idriss, feeling very pleased with himself. A few minutes later Idriss and Mustapha were once more standing in front of King Rachid and Princess Aliya.

'Very well,' said the king to Idriss. 'Please empty your sack at my feet.'

Idriss picked up his small sack. Loosening the top he turned it upside down. Immediately a pile of precious jewels slid out onto the floor. Diamonds, pearls and emeralds glittered from the heap.

'Fantastic,' thought Idriss. 'If this is what is in the small sack, think what will be in the big sack!'

'Thank you,' said the king. 'Now Mustapha, your sack please.'

Dragging his big heavy sack forward, Mustapha untied the top and tipped it up. A pile of heavy bricks and stones clattered out onto the palace floor. Everybody except the king gasped.

'Thank you gentlemen,' said the king. 'Mustapha, I am delighted that you will be the man to marry my daughter. A man who keeps the smallest for himself and gives away the biggest will make a good son-in-law. Remember now, you may both return to the caves I sent you to and you can keep what lies in the sacks there.'

Mustapha smiled. Idriss groaned – he knew what would be in his large sack. Can you guess what it was?

Prayer
Let us pray this morning for wisdom so that we make the right choices in our lives. Let us learn how foolish it is to be selfish.

Hymn
'God knows me' (*Come and Praise* No 15)

Information for the teacher
1   The Biblical figure always associated with wisdom is Solomon. The story of his judgement concerning the two women claiming parenthood of a child is appropriate for use here. It can be found in 1 Kings 3: 16–28.

2   A useful Buddhist saying for use with this story might be: 'All that we are – is the result of what we have thought.' (Dhammapada)

Helicopter rescue   *Qualities*

Introduction
We often see helicopters on television. Sometimes they are helping to save people who are trapped on cliffs or in the sea. This morning's story is about how three men in a helicopter saved the lives of nine other men. The story begins when a ship catches fire . . .

Story
'Lower the lifeboat, men!' shouted the captain of the small ship as the flames

leapt higher and higher. They had to get away from the blazing ship as soon as possible.

The crew scrambled to get into the lifeboat. Once it was in the water they felt safer. But then they got another shock.

'The oars have gone', cried one of them.

'We can't row away from the ship,' muttered another.

Silently they sat and watched as the lifeboat drifted back towards the burning ship.

'Any minute now that ship is gong to blow up,' shouted the captain.

It was then that they heard the sound of the RAF helicopter overhead. Looking up they saw a man lean out, and they heard him shout.

'We've lost our oars,' shouted back the captain.

The helicopter came lower. Then a rope started to come down from it. On the end of the rope was man. The sailors reached out to grab him as he came towards the boat.

'Thanks a lot,' shouted the man, whose name was John. He told the sailors what to do.

'Look,' he said. 'We're going to lift you off this lifeboat one at a time. You get into this harness on the end of the rope, then my friend in the helicopter will wind in the rope and you'll soon be up there. Then you will be safe.'

The sea made the little boat bob up and down. The men could feel the terrible heat from the burning ship, as they got nearer to it.

'Go on,' shouted John, and the first of the sailors dangled and jerked upwards on the rope. When he got to the helicopter's open door hands reached out and helped him inside. Then the rope was lowered to the lifeboat again.

'Next,' shouted John, helping the next sailor into the harness.

Nine times John helped the sailors as the rope pulled them up to the safety of the helicopter. Finally he was alone in the lifeboat.

By now the blazing ship was almost on top of John. As the rope came down from the helicopter the pitching sea and the roaring flames made it very hard for him to catch it. The first time he made a grab he nearly fell overboard. Next time the rope swung wildly over his head.

'I've just got to get it this time,' muttered John, and he gritted his teeth with determination. The rope came swinging down again.

'Now!' he thought and made a desperate grab. He caught the rope in one hand, then managed to get the other hand onto it. There was nobody to help him get into the harness. He would just have to hang on and hope for the best.

Inch by inch the rope was wound upwards. John's arms ached as he clung to it. Then, when he felt he could hang on no longer, he was alongside the helicopter. Friendly arms helped him inside. A great cheer went up from the sailors who were all aboard.

'Great work John,' said the captain of the ship. 'You saved all our lives.' At that moment there was a terrific explosion below as the ship blew up. They had got away just in time!

Later, when the Queen heard about John's bravery, he was awarded a special medal.

Prayer
Let us pray this morning for travellers – in aeroplanes, on ships, in buses, trains or cars. Let us also give thanks for those who come to the rescue when there is an accident.

Hymn
'He who would valiant be' (*Come and Praise* No 44)

Information for the teacher
1   This helicopter rescue took place in the Persian Gulf. 'John' was Seargeant John Glanvill and he was awarded the Air Force Medal for his courage. The other two members of the helicopter crew, Flight Lieutenant Kenneth Lloyd and Flying Officer Maurice Bennee were awarded the Queen's Commendation for valuable service in the air.

2   It might be interesting to consider other forms of rescue. A set of children's cards on working dogs, including some very useful material on Search and Rescue dogs, can be obtained from:
Pedigree Petfoods Education Centre, Walham-on-the-Wolds, Melton Mowbray, Leicestershire
    Two other useful addresses are:
Royal National Lifeboat Institution, West Quay Road, Poole, Dorset B15 1HZ
St John Ambulance Brigade, 1 Grosvenor Crescent, London SW1X 7EF

The flying supper   *Qualities*

Introduction
All of us get disappointed at some time in our lives. For instance, it is very disappointing if you are looking forward to a trip to the seaside but feel ill and can't go. It is disappointing if one of your friends has a party and you don't get invited.

This morning's story is about a man who was looking forward to a really tasty supper – and how he was disappointed. The story took place a long time ago in a far off, hot country – where there are some very greedy birds called kites.

Story

'That looks delicious,' said Nasr-ud-Din.

He was looking in a butcher's shop and he saw a beautiful piece of meat which would be lovely for his supper. Nasr-ud-Din loved food and his wife was a very good cook. Going into the shop he bought the piece of meat.

'You'll enjoy that,' said the butcher.

'I certainly will,' replied Nasr-ud-Din. 'My wife is a terrific cook. She'll take that piece of meat and she'll cook it with herbs and . . . '

'Yes, yes,' interrupted the butcher who knew that once Nasr-ud-Din got talking about his wife's cooking it was hard to stop him. Wrapping up the meat he put it into the old man's basket.

'Mmm, I can hardly wait,' muttered Nasr-ud-Din as he hurried home.

Meanwhile in the sky above the old man was a greedy bird called a kite. It circled around looking for something to eat. The smell of the meat drifted upwards and the kite saw that it was lying in a basket which had no lid on.

'Aha,' thought the kite. 'That old man down there is carrying a lovely piece of meat in that basket. If I wait my chance I'll be able to snatch it away from him and then – bingo – off with the paper and I'll have a splendid supper.'

Nasr-ud-Din was nearly home. It had been a long day and he was tired. Now that the sun was sinking how nice it would be to sit in the courtyard of his house and enjoy a meal with his wife. Before he knew it he was outside his front door. He put his basket on the ground so that he could get his key from his pocket.

That was the moment the kite had been waiting for. With the speed of a dive bomber and with the wind whistling over its wings it swooped down on the basket. Before Nasr-ud-Din could do a thing there was a flurry of wings, a flash of movement – and then the kite was soaring back into the sky – with the meat firmly held in its large beak.

For a moment the disappointment was almost more than Nasr-ud-Din could bear. His lovely supper was now disappearing across the evening sky. An angry frown crossed his face . . . and then . . . he smiled.

'Ha!' he cried at the disappearing bird. 'You have my meat but what is the good of that without my wife's lovely recipe to go with it!'

If there was one thing Nasr-ud-Din had learned in his long life it was that there were always disappointments – and it was always better to try and look on the bright side of things.

Prayer

Help us O God, to bear well the things which are hard to bear.
Help me to bear
   Pain with cheerfulness and without complaint;
   Failure with the perseverance to go on trying until I succeed;
   Disappointment without bitterness and without resentment;
   Delays with the patience which has learned to wait.

William Barclay

Hymn

'Lost and found' (*Come and Praise* No 57)

Information for the teacher

1   Nasr-ud-Din is the central character in many Turkish folk tales. He is often in difficulties but endears himself to the reader (or listener) by his ever-ready wit, quickness of mind and sense of humour.

2   Disappointment and complaint are closely linked and there are many 'sayings' to focus thought in these areas, eg: 'I was sorry I had no gloves until I met a man who had no fingers.'

30.9.87

Isn't that lovely!

Qualities

Introduction

To keep our school looking neat and tidy we have to take care of it. One way of doing this is to make sure that we don't throw sweet papers or other litter about. This morning's story is about a lady called Mrs Pringle who hated to see places looking untidy, or not as nice as they could look. So she decided to do something about it.

Story

Mrs Pringle had to do a lot of travelling. She would get up early in the morning, pack her case and go to the station. There she would get on a train. Sometimes it went north, sometimes south, sometimes east, sometimes west. But whichever way the train went, Mrs Pringle always looked out of the window.

'Look at those lovely trees,' she would say to the other people in her carriage, or, 'What beautiful gardens those houses have.'

On lots of her journeys, however, she looked outside and thought to herself: 'How dreary it looks out there. The grass is brown and dirty and there's not a bit of colour anywhere. I wish I could do something to brighten it up.' Then she had an idea.

Next day Mrs Pringle went to a shop which sold seeds.

'I want some flower seeds please,' she said to the shopkeeper.

'Certainly,' he replied, 'What sort would you like?'

Twenty packets of foxgloves please,' said Mrs Pringle.

The shopkeeper looked surprised.

'You must have a very big garden,' he said.

'Oh I have,' replied Mrs Pringle with a smile, 'very, very big!'

Next day Mrs Pringle was off one one of her journeys again. This time she took a packet of foxglove seeds with her.

After some time the train came to one of the dreary, dirty banks beside the railway track which Mrs Pringle hated so much. The train always went slowly at this point, and always stopped for a short time. When it had stopped, Mrs Pringle carefully opened the window. She looked to see if it was safe and then she threw some of her foxglove seeds into the air. The wind swirled them away onto the bank.

'I do hope some of them grow,' she said to herself.

The next day Mrs Pringle made a journey in another direction. Again she threw a packetful of seeds out of the window. Every day she did the same thing until her twenty packets of seeds were all used up.

Then she waited . . . and waited . . . until on those dreary banks little patches of flowers began to appear.

People sitting in trains with her began to look outside and say: 'Look – isn't that lovely!'

When Mrs Pringle heard this she smiled – and went on buying her packets of flower seeds.

(based on a letter in a woman's magazine)

Prayer

Let us give thanks this morning for those people who keep our towns and villages clean; for gardeners who help to keep parks looking beautiful; for the people who work hard to keep our schools clean and tidy.

Let us always remember not to throw litter or do anything which harms flowers, trees, bushes or bird's nests.

Let us give thanks for all who try to keep our country a beautiful place in which to live.

Hymn

'Think of a world without any flowers' (*Come and Praise* No 17)

Information for the teacher

1   This would be a good opportunity to talk about caring for the environment, for example not picking wild flowers.

2   Many flowers have symbolic connections: a red carnation denotes love; a daisy symbolises the innocence of children; a hyacinth denotes peace of mind; a lily symbolises purity; a rose is the symbol of victory and pride and a violet represents humility.

3   Following Mrs Pringle's example, it might be possible to plant flowers somewhere in the school grounds.

4   Two useful addresses for reference are:
Friends of the Earth, 9 Poland Street, London W1V 2DG.
Keep Britain Tidy Group, Bostel House, 37 West Street, Brighton BN1 2RE.

A brave driver   *Qualities*

Introduction

I expect most of you have seen pictures of black and white American Highway Patrol cars on television. This morning's story is about a man called Chuck who drives one of these cars.

Story

'It's lovely up here,' thought Chuck to himself as he wound the window of his patrol car down. A cool breeze blew in through the window and, parked high up on the mountain road, he gazed down at the scenery below.

'That's strange . . . ' he muttered. Through his open window he heard the noise of a lorry's engine screaming as it raced far too fast. No sooner had he thought this than Chuck saw a lorry hurtling towards him down the steep mountain road. As he sat in his car in the layby he saw the lorry driver's terrified face as it flashed past.

'He's in trouble,' thought Chuck. 'His brakes aren't working.'

Switching his engine on, Chuck slammed his foot on the accelerator and set off downhill after the lorry. Racing as fast as he could he soon caught up with it and when he did so he was horrified when he saw what was written on the back: *Highly dangerous.* Chuck then realised that the lorry was an oil tanker. If it crashed there would be a terrible accident, and the fuel might explode. He had to stop it!

'But how?' he wondered, as the horns of cars coming the other way hooted in fright. 'There's only one thing to do.'

Chuck tried to see round the lorry. When the road was clear, he swung out and went faster until he got in front of the lorry.

'Now for the tricky bit,' he thought to himself. Slowing his car down just a little bit he let the lorry get nearer until it was just touching the back of his car. Then he gradually put his brakes on. Immediately there was a terrible smell of burning rubber. Chuck put his car into a lower gear and then pressed the brakes again. He could feel the huge weight of the lorry forcing him forward, he could smell the brakes burning – but he could also feel the lorry slowing down!

Gradually, as the two vehicles hurtled down the mountain road, Chuck kept pressing his brakes and bit by bit both car and lorry slowed. By now the road was beginning to level out and Chuck could see the first traffic lights of the town which lay in the valley.

'It's got to be *now!*' he shouted out loud. Slamming his foot on the brake he strained to hold the steering wheel steady with all his strength. The smell of burning rubber was dreadful and there was a terrible shrieking, skidding noise as the tyres bit into the road. Then . . . the car, and the lorry came to a stop!

Drenched in sweat Chuck looked through his driving mirror to see the lorry driver slump exhausted over his steering wheel. He'd done it!

When the people of the nearby town of San Bernadino heard the story of Chuck's bravery he was given a medal. He certainly deserved it because he had saved many people's lives.

Prayer

Let us pray this morning for heroes, those people who do incredibly brave deeds to save the lives of others. Let us think particularly this morning of all those who work hard to make our roads safer places.

Hymn
'When a knight won his spurs' (*Come and Praise* No 50)

Information for the teacher

The officer concerned in this incident was called Chuck Downing and he used his patrol car to stop a runaway lorry which was heading for the Californian town of San Bernadino. Most of the driving was done at speeds in excess of 140 kilometres per hour and Officer Downing was able to stop the lorry just a few metres short of the first set of traffic lights in the town.

The wedding party   *Qualities*

Introduction

When somebody gets married there is usually a party. Perhaps some of you have been to a wedding and know about this. Tables are set out with lovely food on them and everybody who has been invited to the party sits down, eats and enjoys themselves. Today's story is about two men who were invited to a wedding party.

Story

Matthew pushed open the door and went into the large room. He was the first person there, which was as he thought it should be. Matthew always liked to be first anywhere.

'Fantastic,' he said to himself. There in front of him was a very long table. Set out on it were plates of cold meat, potatoes and other vegetables, trifles and cakes. As he was first, all the seats round the table were empty.

'Mmmmm – that looks terrific,' thought Matthew. 'Now where am I going to sit?'

He looked again at the table and then he was sure where he ought to go.

'An important man like me will be sure to get one of the best seats. I'll sit as near as I can to the bride and bridegroom.'

No sooner had Matthew taken his place than Peter came into the room.

'That looks marvellous,' thought Peter to himself. 'I'm sure everybody is going to enjoy this party. Now . . . where shall I sit? Well, I'm not a very important guest – I'll sit right at the bottom of the table. I'll leave those places for important people near the bride and bridegroom.'

Gradually more and more guests came in and the seats round the table began to fill up. Ladies with beautiful hats and men in their best suits smiled at each other and found seats. Then the bride's father came into the room. He was in charge of the wedding party.

'Now I hope everybody has found a seat and been sensible about it. Oh no – just look where Peter is. He is one of John's best friends – he can't sit right down there. I must change his seat.'

So the bride's father went up to Peter.

'Hello Mr Larkins,' said Peter. 'It looks as if it is going to be a very good party.'

'Yes, yes,' said Mr Larkins, 'but you can't sit here Peter. John asked me to make sure that you had a seat near him.'

'Oh but . . . '

'Come along please,' said Mr Larkins.

He then took Peter right to the top of the table where Matthew was sitting.

'I'm very sorry sir,' he said, 'but your seat is for a very special guest. Would you mind changing please?'

So Matthew had to go down to the last place on the table.

Prayer
Let us think this morning about the way we behave. Let us not be the sort of people who always push their way in and try to be first everywhere. Let us think about others before we think about ourselves.

Hymn
'God has promised' (*Come and Praise* No 31)

Information for the teacher
1 A modest person is described in the dictionary as being one who is 'unobtrusive, unpretentious, unassuming, decent, moderate, not excessive or extreme.' Such qualities, obviously in appropriate language, could be discussed in conjunction with this story.

2 Weddings often feature in the Bible. A common theme is that an invitation to a wedding was very special and to decline it was considered an insult (Matthew 22: 1–13). Great preparations were involved in weddings; the parable of the ten virgins and and the oil for their lamps could be used here (Matthew 25: 10–12).

Would you like to be rich?
Qualities

Introduction
Would you like to be rich? If somebody asked you that question I expect you would say, 'Yes please!'

This morning's story took place a long time ago. It is about a poor farmer called Shimon, and what happened when an old man said to him: 'Would you like to be rich?'

Story
Shimon was a poor farmer. One day he was at work in his fields when an old man came by.

'Good morning,' said the old man.

'Good morning,' replied Shimon.

'How would you like to be rich?' asked the old man.

'I'm too busy to answer riddles,' replied Shimon. 'Sorry, but I must get on with my work.'

'Oh it's not a riddle,' went on the old man. 'I've come to make you an offer. You can be rich for the next seven years – or you can choose to be rich in your old age. A warning though – you'll have to pay back the money I give you now if you choose to be rich right away.'

'You're not joking, are you?' asked Shimon.

The old man shook his head, so Shimon asked him to wait and he hurried back to the farm house to talk over the decision with his wife.

'Well,' he said when he got back. 'My wife and I have decided we would like to be rich now.'

'So be it,' said the old man, and went on his way.

Shimon started his ploughing again and immediately his plough hit something in the ground – it was a sack full of gold coins! He staggered home with this treasure, and met his wife running out of the house.

'The bedroom, the bedroom!' she cried, 'Its full of sacks of gold!'

That night Shimon and his wife talked about their good fortune.

'There's no doubt about it,' said Shimon, 'we've got to share our good luck with all those other poor people we know.'

So next day they took some of the gold and gave it to the beggars in the market place. They helped other poor farmers buy tools; they gave meals to hungry travellers; they gave money to the homeless so that they could find somewhere to live; they paid for the repair of poor friends' homes.

The years slipped by. Shimon and his wife were tremendously happy at being able to help so many people. They still worked hard themselves and they were liked by everybody who knew them.

Then, one day, the old man came back.

'Well,' he said, 'I hope you enjoyed the money. I've come to take it back now.'

'Hmm,' said Shimon, 'it's not quite as easy as that I'm afraid.'

He then explained how all the money had been given away. When he had finished the old man smiled.

'So – you are honest as well,' he said. 'I already know what you have done with the money because so many people have told me how kind you have been. I don't want the money back because you have used it so well. What a better place the world would be if others were as kind as you.'

So saying the old man went on his way.

(adapted from an old Jewish folk tale)

Prayer
This morning's prayer was made up by a saint. He said that to be happy and

contented we should: 'Give and not count the cost; work without looking for rest and reward.'

(adapted from St. Ignatius)

Hymn
'The best gift' (*Come and Praise* No 59)

Information for the teacher
1   It is significant that this story allows for seven rich years because seven was the Hebrew sacred number – perhaps because the seventh day ended the creation cycle and became the Sabbath. The story of Joseph and the seven lean/prosperous years would also be useful here.

2   The Talmud, a very important book to Jews, is like an encyclopedia of the religion and contains many proverbs and parables.

With help from Wendy
Creatures

Introduction
Dogs are a bit like people. Some are noisy, some are shy, some are friendly, some are bouncy. This morning's story is about a little terrier called Wendy. Now Wendy was a very nervous dog. She had been a stray as a puppy, but the RSPCA found her a good home by the time she was twelve months old. Even though she was well looked after Wendy was still very nervous.

Story
'I'm going to take Wendy out for a walk, Mum,' shouted nine-year-old Nigel to his mother.

'All right dear, but be careful of the traffic.'

'That's one reason I'm taking her – to see if she can get used to it.'

Wendy was terribly nervous in traffic and Nigel was doing his best to help her get over this nervousness.

'We'll soon be away from these cars,' said Nigel to Wendy, 'and then we'll have some fun.'

Minutes later they were charging down the bank of a beach near where they lives when – it happened!

Nigel slipped and plunged down the bank. When he reached the bottom and tried to get up he couldn't. He had landed in some thick treacherous mud called a quagmire. The harder Nigel tried to get out of this quagmire the more he sank back into it. Soon only his head and shoulders could be seen. He was trapped!

All the time Wendy watched. She was terrified. Then suddenly she turned round and ran up the bank, back to where the traffic was busiest. The nervous little dog waited, and then dashed across the road. Soon, dirty and panting, she was home again.

'Wendy – where's Nigel?' asked Nigel's mother.

Wendy barked and barked and barked, and ran towards the door.

'That's not like you Wendy . . . you want us to follow you, don't you?'

The little dog barked even more loudly and within a minute Mr and Mrs Bolding were following her in search of Nigel.

Bounding ahead of them the little dog kept up a constant barking to make sure they were following. Mr and Mrs Bolding were amazed when their nervous pet led them through heavy traffic to the beach with the quagmire at the bottom.

They were just about there when they saw a man and lady dragging Nigel from the clinging mud. Mrs Bolding let out a gasp and dashed towards her mud-covered son.

'Nigel! . . . Oh thank you, thank you!' she cried to the rescuers.

'I reckon it's this little dog you ought to thank,' said the man. 'If we hadn't heard him barking so much we wouldn't have come over here. Then we saw him dash off and we reckoned he'd gone for help. Some dog that!'

'Oh Wendy,' cried a muddy Nigel, and his mum and dad.

'She saved my life,' said Nigel.

Wendy gave another bark – but this time it sounded quite different!

Prayer
Thank you Lord for all animals. Let us say a special prayer this morning for the RSPCA – the Royal Society for the Prevention of Cruelty to Animals. Let us give thanks for the care and protection it gives to helpless, lost or injured animals.

Hymn
'Cross over the road' (*Come and Praise* No 70)

Information for the teacher
1   This story is based on a real-life incident. It could lead on to a consideration of other dog heroes (or heroines). Britain's animal VC is the Dickin Medal, instituted by Mrs Maria Dickin in 1943. Accounts of dog winners of this medal can be found in *The Guinness Book of Pet Records* by Gerald L Wood (Guinness, 1984).

2   In following up the theme of accidents a useful address is:
Royal Society for the Prevention of Accidents, Cannon House, The
Priory, Queensway, Birmingham B4 6BS

3   The RSPCA produces a variety of publications about pet care and animal
welfare; there is also a Junior Membership Scheme. Contact:
Royal Society for the Protection of Animals, The Causeway, Horsham,
West Sussex RH12 1HG

Red, white and yellow   *Creatures*

Introduction
Sometimes stories about animals, birds and insects tell us a lot about how
human beings behave towards each other. I think you will see what I mean
if you listen carefully to this morning's story.

Story
There were once three butterflies who were great friends. They enjoyed
fluttering and dancing in the sunshine. They were always cheerful and very
happy together.

One day they were a long way from home when a terrific rainstorm started.

'We must find some shelter,' they all cried. Then they saw a flower nearby.
It was a tall white lily. They flew towards it.

'Will you shelter us until the rain passes please?' they all cried.

The lily looked at the butterflies, noticing that one was white, one was
red and one was yellow.

'I'll shelter *you*,' said the lily, nodding at the white butterfly, 'because you
are the same colour as me. But I don't want the other two.'

'Then you certainly won't have me!' replied the white butterfly angrily.
'I'll stay with my friends thank you very much.'

Whirling round in the rain the butterfly friends then saw a tulip. Flying
towards it they asked for shelter again.

'Hmmmm,' said the tulip, 'well there are red tulips and yellow tulips but
no white ones. So you two, red and yellow, are welcome, but there is no
room for you, white, I'm afraid.'

'Then we are certainly not coming in,' said the red and yellow butterflies
together, and all three flew off again.

This time they had no sooner started their search for shelter when the clouds blew away, the rain stopped, and the sun came out. Smiling down and drying the butterflies' glistening wings it smiled in pleasure.

'Well done, my friends,' said the sun. 'Well done.'

(adapted from a German folk tale)

Prayer

Let us think this morning about bottles. The shape, size and colour of bottles doesn't really matter – it is what is inside them that really counts. Let us remember it is just the same with people.

Hymn

'Black and white' (*Come and Praise* No 67)

Information for the teacher

1   The hymn for this assembly makes a useful focus for discussing and considering this difficult subject. It would be particularly useful to link it with hymn 68 from the same source ('Kum ba yah') in talking about how people's needs transcend their colour.

2   An organisation which distributes a great deal of useful multi-ethnic material is:
Commission for Racial Equality, Education Office, Elliot House, 10–12 Allington Street, London SW1E 5EN

3   A further development of this theme is a consideration of conscience – which in the Biblical sense is the voice of God encouraging the 'right' and condemning the 'wrong'. 1 Peter 3:21 stresses the importance of baptism in cleansing the sins which make us have a bad conscience.

How the kingfisher got its name   *Creatures*

Introduction

This morning's story was first told in India many, many years ago. The story is about two birds, a king, a princess and a golden ring.

Story

The two birds lived very near to each other. One of them, who we will call 'the fisher', was coloured blue, white and brown. The other was a crow, whose feathers were not nearly so pretty. The crow was very jealous of the fisher.

'I wish I had feathers the same colour as that fisher,' thought the crow. 'And I wish I could dive down to the water and catch fish as easily as she does.'

The fisher did not know that the crow was jealous and she was always very friendly.

'Good morning Mrs Crow,' said the fisher one morning. 'I see you've got a nest full of eggs just like me. We'll soon have our babies now.'

'Hmmm,' grunted the crow, and then she had a brilliant idea!

'While that bird is catching fish,' thought the crow, 'I'll change her eggs for mine – and then at least I'll have babies with lovely coloured feathers.'

The crow did this and soon afterwards the two sets of babies were born. Immediately the fisher knew something was wrong – and she went to see the crow.

'I think something has gone wrong,' said the fisher. 'You have got my babies, and I have got yours.'

'Nonsense!' said the crow. 'These are my babies – now go away and leave me alone.'

The fisher was very upset, but she didn't know what to do. As she was sitting on the branch of a tree thinking, she heard someone crying. Looking down she saw that it was the king's daughter.

'Your Highness,' the fisher said to the princess, 'you seem very upset. Is there anything I can do to help?'

'Oh dear, it's awful,' said the princess. 'I was taking a walk by the river when I accidentally dropped my gold ring into the water. It was a special present from my father the king and I know that he will be as upset as I am that it is lost. Oh dear.'

'Don't worry,' said the fisher. 'I'll see if I can help.'

The fisher then flew away over the river. Swooping down low, she looked into the calm water. Suddenly she saw something twinkle from the mud at the bottom of the river. Diving down she slid gracefully through the water and then flew up into the air with the twinkling object in her beak. It was the lost gold ring!

A few minutes later the fisher was back to where she had left the princess. By now the king and many of his servants were there too. The little bird swooped down and dropped the ring in the palm of the princess's outstretched hand.

'Oh thank you, little bird, that's wonderful!' said the princess.

'It certainly is,' exclaimed the King. 'Is there anything I can do for you in return?'

'Well . . . ' said the fisher, and then she told him how the crow had stolen her eggs.

Shortly afterwards the king was talking to both the fisher and the crow.

'You should be ashamed of yourself,' said the king to the crow. 'Fancy taking someone else's eggs and then saying the babies were yours. Return them at once – and take much more care of your own babies!'

The crow felt very ashamed for the way she had behaved.

The king then turned to the fisher.

'Thank you so much for your help my friend,' he said. 'From now on you will have a special name. You will be called the *KING*fisher.'

(a very free adaptation of a story by S G Potham in Indian Folk Tales
Sabbash Publishers)

Prayer
Let us think this morning about how upset we are if we think we have been unfairly treated. Let us pray that we are never tempted to do unfair or unkind things ourselves. Let us remember that one good turn deserves another.

Hymn
'God knows me' (*Come and Praise* No 15)

Information for the teacher
Many folk tales use birds to symbolise human virtues, foibles and frailties. Perhaps in connection with this assembly some comment on the 'wisest' of all birds might be appropriate:

'The wise old owl sat high in an oak,
And the more he heard the less he spoke,
The less he spoke the more he heard,
So why can't we be like that wise old bird?'

(Anon)

A cat has nine lives   *Creatures*

Introduction
Did you know that a cat is supposed to have nine lives? Nobody really knows how this strange idea first came about – but it might have been because of the following story.

This story is about Hans, an old woodcutter who lived in the Black Forest in Germany, long, long ago. Hans was a very poor man, and he lived in a small, rather tumbledown cottage.

Story

'Ah well, another day's work done,' thought Hans to himself as he walked through the wood to his poor little cottage. He reached the cottage and was just about to open the door when he glimpsed a sudden movement out of the corner of his eye.

'Why,' gasped Hans, 'it's a kitten.'

Bending down he picked up the nervous little kitten and cradled it in his arms.

'You've come to the wrong house, my little pet,' he said. 'I've got hardly enough food to feed myself, never mind you as well. However – let's see what we've got.'

So Hans shared out the tiny bit of food he had between the kitten and himself, and it spent the night lying cosily by his fireside. Next morning Hans got ready to go to work.

'Now little kitten, I'll take you to the crossroads in the wood. Somebody who is a lot better off than me is sure to find you there and give you a good home.'

Rather sadly Hans did this and then went off to where he was chopping down trees. That night, tired and hungry, he got home – to find the kitten on his doorstep again.

'Oh you poor little fellow,' he said. 'I've got even less to eat tonight than I had last night. Never mind, we'll share it.'

The next morning Hans took the kitten to the crossroads again. He was sad to leave it but he hoped somebody would come along and give it a good home. But that night, when he got back to his cottage, there was his tiny little friend.

Nine times Hans fed the kitten, kept it for the night, and then took it to the crossroads. Nine times it came back. After the ninth time Hans scratched his head, took the kitten in his arms and tickled it under the chin.

'Well it looks as if you are determined to stay,' he said. 'I don't know why – I can't feed you very well and you'll never have any company because I'm out all day and every day from sunrise to sunset. However, if you want to stay I'll be pleased to share whatever I have with you.'

So Hans made a proper little bed for the kitten and he shared whatever food he had with it. Then, strange things began to happen. A rich lady called at his cottage and asked Hans if he could make a cradle for her baby. Hans was very good at working with wood but nobody had ever asked him to make anything before. The cradle he made for the lady was beautiful and she was delighted with it. When she paid him for it she went off and told all her friends about what a good carpenter the old man who lived in the wood was. Soon many people visited Hans' cottage. They asked him to make more cradles, and tables and chairs – and soon Hans became quite rich.

Meanwhile the kitten grew into a fine, friendly cat and the two of them were very happy. One day an old friend who had known him when he was poor asked Hans how it had all happened.

'It's a funny thing,' said Hans, 'but my luck seemed to change when I decided to keep my friend Oscar here. I gave him nine chances to find a better home but he always came back here.'

Prayer
Let us think this morning about how we are sometimes given more than one chance to do the right thing. Let us pray that when we make mistakes we have the chance of putting them right.

Hymn
'All creatures of our God and King' (*Come and Praise* No 7)

Information for the teacher
1   In Christian symbolism 9 is considered an angelic number because the Bible speaks of nine choirs of angels.

2   This story is a good illustration of the motto 'If at first you don't succeed, try, try again'. A useful Bible reference might be Luke 18: 1–6.

A famous dog   *Creatures*

Introduction
This morning's story is about one of the most famous dogs who ever lived. He was a small Skye terrier, and his name was Bobby. His story begins in the Scottish city of Edinburgh over a hundred years ago.

Story
Every Wednesday in Edinburgh there was a busy market. People came from all over the city to buy and sell. Among them was a man called Mr Gray, and his Skye terrier, Bobby.

'You never see that man without his little dog,' everyone used to say.

Now at one o'clock every day a gun was fired from Edinburgh castle. Whenever he heard the gun, Bobby pricked up his ears because he knew that meant dinner time. Mr Gray would head for his favourite café with Bobby following.

'Good morning Mr Gray,' said Mr Traill who owned the café.

'Morning Mr Traill,' replied Mr Gray, 'the usual please.'

Then, while Mr Gray was having his dinner, Bobby would be given a bun and a bone and he would eat these sitting at his master's feet. Year after year this went on and then, suddenly, Mr Gray died. He was buried in a cemetery called Greyfriars and Bobby was given another home.

The very next Wednesday however, Mr Traill got quite a shock in his café. Shortly after the one o'clock gun was fired at the castle, his café door was pushed open and in trotted a very scruffy looking Bobby.

'Bobby!' exclaimed Mr Traill. 'What are you doing here? Well you'd better have your dinner I suppose.'

He gave Bobby a big bread bun – and then he got another surprise! Picking up the bun, Bobby hurried out and went straight to Greyfriars cemetery where he sat beside Mr Gray's grave and ate his dinner. Bobby stayed by the grave all that day and night. The next day he arrived at the café just after one o'clock and did the same thing again . . . and the next day . . . and the next . . . .

The people who now owned Bobby were very worried about him but every time they bought him back he ran away again. The cemetery keeper said that dogs were not allowed in the cemetery and he tried to stop Bobby getting in – but when the gate was closed Bobby just scrambled over the fence.

By now, everybody in Edinburgh had heard about Bobby and they decided that he would have to be helped. Mr Traill continued to give him his dinner at one o'clock every day when he called and some other kind people gave him a kennel to sleep in beside his master's grave.

Soon the whole city watched out for him.

'There's Bobby,' people said as he went into the café.

'Bobby's on his way home,' pointed others as Bobby headed back to Greyfriars.

For 14 years this loyal little dog guarded his master's grave and by now the people of Edinburgh not only knew him, but they loved him very much. Finally Bobby died in 1872. He was buried at Greyfriars cemetery, near his master.

If you go to Edinburgh, you can see Bobby's grave, and if you go to the museum there you can see his collar. What's more, in the city centre there is a fountain and sitting on top of it is a statue of Bobby – one of the world's best loved and most famous dogs.

Prayer

Thank you, God, for the loyalty and friendship of dogs who are our pets. Let us try to deserve the way they care about us.

Hymn
'My faith is an oaken staff' (*Come and Praise* No 46)

Information for the teacher
1   Mr Gray was a Midlothian farmer who travelled to Edinburgh every Wednesday for the market. Bobby's collar was presented to him by the Lord Provost of Edinburgh in 1857. The collar and Bobby's dinner bowl can now be seen in the Huntly Museum, Edinburgh.

2   The story is re-told in *Greyfriars Bobby* by Lavinia Derwent, (Puffin, 1985).

3   A useful selection of stories about the devotion of dogs can be found in *The Guinness Book of Pet Records* by Gerald L Wood (Guinness, 1984).

Using the gifts God gave us   *Creatures*

Introduction
I expect all of you like solving puzzles and doing tricks. To do these things we have to think hard and work things out. This morning's story is about a crow. He had to solve a puzzle to stay alive – this is how he did it.

Story
Cornelius was a crow and he lived in a country where it sometimes got very hot indeed. One day he was flying across a brilliant blue sky. The sun scorched down on his feathers and he felt absolutely exhausted.

'If I don't get a drink soon I think I'll die,' he said to himself. 'There's just nothing to drink down there.'

As he said this he looked at the dry, pebbly ground beneath him. All the rivers had dried up and there wasn't a drop of water to be seen anywhere. Then the desperate bird spotted something unusual.

'That's strange,' he thought. 'I wonder what that is? I'd better fly down and find out.'

Tiredly flying down to investigate, Cornelius landed beside – a bottle.

'There's no doubt about it,' he said to himself. 'That's water in there.'

Cornelius could see that the bottle, which had no top on, was half filled with water. But – how was he going to get a drink from it? The top of the bottle was too narrow to put his head in. Even if he had been able to squeeze in, he couldn't reach the water. If he knocked the bottle over so that the water ran out, it would all drain away into the ground before he could drink it.

'This is a puzzle,' thought Cornelius. 'What am I do do?'

He looked round about. For as far as he could see there was just dry, stony ground and lots of little pebbles . . . little . . . pebbles. Suddenly, Cornelius had an idea!

Bending his head he picked up a small pebble. Then, fluttering to the neck of the bottle, he dropped it in. He did the same with another pebble, and another, and . . . .

As each pebble dropped into the bottle the water began to rise. It got nearer and nearer to the top until eventually it was high enough for Cornelius to dip his beak in and enjoy a beautiful, life-saving drink.

Cornelius had solved the puzzle, and saved his life, by using the gifts God gave him.

(adapted from Aesop)

Prayer

Gifts
Blue, blue, blue is the sky,
Green, green, green is the grass,
Tall, tall, tall is the tree,
Given to you and given to me.
God made the world, He worked to a plan.
In it he created a woman and man.
'Now,' He said, 'the world is for free,
All that I ask is believe in Me.'

Olive Kershaw

Hymn
'The best gift' (*Come and Praise* No 59)

Information for the teacher
'Gifts' in the sense of this story can be seen as 'Talents' in the Biblical sense. The famous parable about talents can be found in Matthew 25: 14–30.

'I don't remember'   Creatures

Introduction
This morning's story is about a man who pretended he couldn't remember

something. He was asked to look after a friend's turkeys and one of them mysteriously disappeared. This is what happened . . .

Story

One day Ali told Farouk that he was going away for a few days holiday.

'Would you be very kind and do me a favour?' asked Ali.

'Certainly, certainly,' said Farouk. 'What is it you want me to do?'

'Well,' said Ali, 'could you please look after my 20 turkeys for me until I get back?'

'Certainly, certainly,' said Farouk, and Ali went off on his holiday.

Now the turkeys were big and fat and Farouk could not resist killing one and eating it.

A week later Ali came back.

'Thank you for looking after my turkeys,' he said to Farouk, and he gave him a small present he had brought back from holiday.

'But . . . ' he went on. 'I left you 20 turkeys to look after and now . . . there are only 19.'

'Really,' said Farouk, 'well I never noticed. I don't remember anything happening to one of them.'

Now Ali was very angry and he went to the headman of the village and asked what could be done.

'Let me think about it,' said the headman. 'You and Farouk come to see me at 9 o'clock tomorrow morning.'

Next morning Ali and Farouk stook in front of the headman.

'Tell me your stories,' he said.

Ali told how he had left 20 turkeys. Farouk said he didn't know how many there had been and he didn't remember anything happening to one of them.

'Bring the turkeys here,' said the headman.

When the turkeys arrived the headman sent for twenty soldiers.

'Now take a turkey each and prepare to kill it,' said the headman to the soldiers. 19 of them picked up a turkey, but for the last soldier there was no turkey.

'I forgot there were only 19,' said the headman. Then he said to the soldier: 'Take *him* instead of a turkey.'

As he said this he pointed to the terrified Farouk, who immediately thought he was going to be killed.

'No, no,' he cried. 'I remember, I remember. There were 20 turkeys . . . I ate one of them.'

'Aaah,' said the headman. He then ordered the soldiers to return the turkeys to Ali, and Farouk promised to pay for the one he had eaten. He never did anything so unkind, deceitful or dishonest again.

(adapted from an old Egyptian folk tale)

Prayer

Let us think this morning about how we often make excuses, or even tell lies, when we have done something we know we shouldn't have done. Let us be brave enough to tell the truth always.

Hymn

'The wise men bring their learning' (*Come and Praise* No 64)

Information for the teacher

The Bible intimates, particularly in its Old Testament stories, that wisdom is acquired through observation, experience and reflection. This theme is also followed up in many folk tales, where wise men are almost always old, shrewd and reflective. Perhaps with young children this theme could be pursued to help them appreciate the wisdom acquired by people such as their grandparents.

Saved by a dog   *Creatures*

Introduction

Long, long ago some people had terrible lives as slaves. If you were a slave you got no wages for your work, you had to do everything your master told you, and you were never allowed to leave his house.

This morning's story is about a slave who escaped – and what happened to him.

Story

'They'll never catch me now,' thought John as he ran across the dark countryside. After years as a slave he had escaped. 'No more beatings from my cruel master,' he thought, as he raced to freedom.

But then it happened . . .

Unable to see in the darkness, John crashed into the low wall which surrounded a well. He fell forward and with a cry plunged down the deep shaft. Fortunately the water had dried up and the well was no longer used, but John was bruised and shocked when he picked himself up at the bottom.

No sooner had he done so than he heard men shouting and dogs barking in the distance.

'They're looking for me,' he thought. 'What a stroke of luck falling in here. I'll just stay quiet until they have finished looking for me and then I'll climb out and get on my way.'

All that night John lay crouched and quiet at the bottom of the well. To make sure he was safe he stayed there for the whole of the next day too. When it was dark again he thought it was time to climb out.

But, try as he might, he couldn't manage it. His fingers couldn't grip hard enough; he couldn't find anywhere to put his feet . . .

'I know,' John thought. 'I'll have to push my feet against one wall and press my back agasint the other and edge up slowly and carefully.'

He set about doing this but after getting only a little way up the wall he fell back again. This happened time after time. All night John tried to climb out of the well. By morning he was tired out and very frightened. He had escaped from being a slave but now he was going to starve to death down a well.

Then, as the first light of morning lit the round opening at the top of the well, John saw a dog looking down at him. It was not one of the savage dogs which had been looking for him, and it seemed friendly.

'I wish you could help me, friend dog,' John called to it.

The dog gave a little bark, and then ran away.

'What could he do to help anyway?' thought John.

It must have been two hours before he noticed the dog standing at the top again. As he watched, it dropped something from its mouth. Reaching out in the dim light John saw that it had dropped a piece of meat to him.

He ate the meat hungrily because he had had no food for two days. The juice of the meat was as good as a drink too. After that, twice every day the dog came and dropped food to John.

Meanwhile the dog's owner wondered what was going on.

'Have you seen what Henry is up to?' he asked his wife. 'Every meal time he eats some of his food – and then he dashes off somewhere with the rest.'

'We'll have to follow him and see where he goes,' said the man's wife.

So the two followed the dog and found John in the well. They used a rope to pull him out and then they listened to his story of how Henry had saved his life. They took John back home with them until he was rested and well fed and then they waved goodbye to him as he went on his way to freedom.

Prayer
May those who are strong care for those who are weak;
May those who are free care for those who are not.
May those who are rich care for those who are poor;
May those who are fortunate care for those who are less so.

Hymn
'All creatures of our God and King' (*Come and Praise* No 7)

Information for the teacher

1   This story, with its background of slavery, escape, being trapped and then saved, could be supplemented by part of a prayer by St Francis. (The words could be altered to make them suitable to the age group.)
'Where there is hatred, let us sow love;
Where there is doubt, faith;
Where there is despair, hope;
Where there is darkness, light;
Where there is sadness, joy.'

2   It was the lifelong mission of William Wilberforce to have slavery abolished. As a Member of Parliament, in 1807, he succeeded in stopping the carriage of slaves in British ships. In July 1833 his aim was achieved and all slaves on British soil were freed. Wilberforce died soon afterwards.

The brave little wren   *Creatures*

Introduction

This morning's story is about winter. This is the time when the trees are bare, cold winds blow, and we need our thick coats on.

But birds don't have thick coats to put on and sometimes winter seems very, very long to them. In fact one year winter seemed so long that the birds decided the sun was never coming back. Listen to what they did about this.

Story

'Somebody will have to go,' said the robin. 'I don't feel the cold as much as the rest of you – but somebody will have to go.'

'He's right,' said the starling.

'Yes, but whoooooo?' hooted the owl.

The birds were all gathered together in the forest. It was winter, but this was no ordinary winter. The cold had bitten deep into everything. Trees were stiff and bare and the birds felt as if they were freezing to death. That was why they were having the meeting – one of them must fly away, find the sun, and bring back some warmth. Then the little wren spoke up.

'I'll go,' she said. 'I'll go and find some warmth for us.'

'How brave you are,' said the sparrow.

'Do take care,' said a big, black and white magpie.

'Caw . . . ' croaked a raven. 'Thank you little wren.'

Then, flapping her wings hurriedly, the wren fluttered off into the cold, dark sky.

'Goodbye, goodbye,' cried all the other birds, and they settled down to wait for her return.

Time passed slowly. The frost grew harder. The wind blew colder.

'We'll never be warm again,' grumbled an old crow.

Then, just when the birds had given up hope, they saw a strange light in the sky.

'Whaaaat is it?' asked the owl.

'It's . . . Jenny, our little wren!' cried the robin.

Slowly the wren flew nearer. The birds could tell that she was very, very tired. They could also see that she was carrying a brightly burning torch.

'Hurray,' they cried, 'welcome home little friend, welcome!'

The wren landed on the ground and the other birds took the torch from her and lit a warm fire. Soon they were all gathered round it chatting with joy at being warm again.

'Well done Jenny,' said the starling, 'Jenny . . . Jenny? . . . Where is she?'

The birds looked round. The little wren lay on the ground at the edge of the crowd. It was only then that they noticed how the burning torch had burnt off all her feathers. She lay there gasping, her heart hardly seeming to beat at all.

'Oh my goodness,' gasped several of the birds. 'Oh dear, what can we do?'

Then a quiet and rather scruffy crow spoke up.

'Our little friend needs some new feathers,' he said. 'Mine aren't very beautiful but . . . '

So saying, he plucked out one of his feathers and laid it on the wren. One by one the other birds did the same. Soon the little wren was warm and rested beneath a warm blanket of feathers.

In time her own feathers grew again, but the birds never forgot how she had helped them in that cold, cold winter.

Prayer

Let us pray today for all those people who help us to keep warm in winter – for those who make our warm clothes; for builders who make our houses; for workers who help us to get gas, electricity and coal to keep our houses light and warm.

Hymn

'Join with us' (*Come and Praise* No 30)

Information for the teacher

1   The sun and the moon feature in many folk stories. There are several

Biblical references to the sun: made by God (Gen 1:16); its help in growth (Deut 33:14); its heat (Ps 121:6).

2   For information about the importance of the sun in various beliefs, stories etc a useful book is: *The Encyclopedia of Myths and Legends of All Nations* by H S Robinson and K Wilson (Kaye Ward 1962).

3   Another possible source for information to link with this story is: Royal Society for the Protection of Birds, The Lodge, Sandy, Beds.

Home for dogs   *Creatures*

Introduction

I wonder how many of you have a dog as a pet? You will know if you do that it has to have plenty of water to drink; regular meals; exercise; a warm basket to sleep in. Can you imagine how awful it would be if your Mum or Dad suddenly said: 'We're not going to keep Roger (or whatever your pet's name is) any longer – and threw it out?

This morning's story took place a long time ago, and it begins with a poor dog who had no home.

Story

Mrs Tealby lived in London a long time ago – 125 years ago, in fact. One day she was walking along the street where she lived when she saw Skippy.

'Oh, there's that poor little dog again,' she thought. 'Poor little Skippy.'

Every day for a week she had seen a small, dirty mongrel sniffing the pavement for scraps of food. Every time he saw her he skipped away nervously – so she called him 'Skippy' to herself.

'If he's always on this street he can't have a home to go to,' thought Mrs Tealby as she walked to her house. 'Poor little chap, I'll see if I can help him.'

When she got home she put some scraps of food on a plate and put it outside her door. Watching through the window she soon saw Skippy sniffing up the path. When he saw the food he wolfed it down as if he had not eaten for a week. Opening the door, Mrs Tealby held out a bowl of water.

'Skippy, Skippy – come and have a drink.'

Skippy came in nervously, drank the water, and then licked Mrs Tealby's hand.

'You poor little chap,' she said, as she stroked his tangled fur and felt how thin he was. 'Nobody cares for you, do they?'

So Mrs Tealby gave Skippy a home. As she walked about the streets of North London where she lived, Mrs Tealby then began to notice more dogs like Skippy. Dogs of all sizes – but all thin, scruffy and hungry.

'Those poor starving dogs,' thought Mrs Tealby, and she began to take more of them into her own home. Soon the people who lived around her found out about this and they started to bring her stray dogs too.

'Have you heard about that kind lady Mrs Tealby?' they said. 'She's started a home for lost and starving dogs you know.'

Eventually the Queen heard about Mrs Tealby and her stray dogs! She told her ministers to give Mrs Tealby some help and a proper home was found for the dogs at a place called Battersea in South London.

Over 100 years later this home for stray dogs is still there. Now vets and other experts take in stray dogs, make sure they are cared for if they are ill, look after them and try to find new homes for them. In the year 1984, 19,850 stray dogs were taken into the Battersea Home. So the good work Mrs Tealby started all those years ago still goes on today.

Prayer
Let us pray that our eyes see things which need to be done and our hands are useful in doing them.

Hymn
'The earth is yours O God' (*Come and Praise* No 6)

Information for the teacher
1   You can find out about current activities at the Battersea Dogs' Home by sending a stamped addressed envelope to:
     The Battersea Dogs' Home, 4 Battersea Park Road, London SW8 4AA.

2   A human parallel to this story could be that of Dr Barnado. Born in Dublin in 1845, Thomas Barnado came to London to study medicine. In the East End he discovered dozens of homeless children and, taking a large house in Stepney, he provided a home for many of them. People heard of his enterprise and gifts of money enabled him to open more houses. He died in 1905 but of course his work still goes on today.

Fritz to the rescue   *Creatures*

Introduction
This morning's story is about Mrs Miller, her children Betty, Jason, Wayne and the baby; and most of all about Fritz, who is a very big Alsatian dog.

The Miller family, and Fritz, lived in a flat high up in a tall building in Chicago, which is a town in America. One day a terrible thing happened . . .

Story

'Mum, Mum, come quick!'

Betty Miller's voice was high and tearful as she called to her mother. Mrs Miller dropped her sewing and ran into the kitchen. What she saw was very frightening – the cooker was on fire!

'What shall we do, Mum?' screamed Betty.

Quickly Mrs Miller threw some water on the blazing cooker – but it was no good. The flames got bigger and bigger.

'We must get out and call the fire brigade,' gasped Mrs Miller. 'Hurry, you get Jason and Wayne.'

Betty ran back into the living room and got her two younger brothers. Mrs Miller grabbed the twins and they rushed downstairs.

The family lived at the top of a block of flats and Mrs Miller knew that there was a telephone on the ground floor. As they hurried down the stairs Fritz, the family dog, bounded along after them.

'Betty, when we get to the bottom you ring the fire brigade – dial 999 – and I'll rush back upstairs and get the baby.'

'Right Mum,' said a frightened but brave Betty.

Soon the family reached the ground floor. Mrs Miller told the three children to wait at the bottom of the stairs while she went back to get the baby. Suddenly there was a Whooooshing noise and flames shot down the staircase. Mrs Miller screamed.

'My baby – he's still upstairs!'

By now lots of people had rushed out of their flats.

'You can't go back up there,' said one of them.

'But I must!'

Just then Fritz barked and jumped up at Mrs Miller's side.

'Fritz – bring baby – quickly!' she gasped.

No sooner had Mrs Miller said this than Fritz, ignoring the flames, bounded back up the stairs. By now the distant siren of a fire engine could be heard and crowds of people were pushing their way out of the flats.

Mrs Miller stayed where she was, gazing anxiously up the stairs. When she had almost given up hope, the huge shape of Fritz the Alsatian appeared through the flames. In his mouth he held the sheet in which Mrs Miller's baby was wrapped.

This story has a happy ending. Mrs Miller's baby was completely unharmed. Poor Fritz was quite badly burned but he did recover after a lot of treatment. When he was better he was awarded a medal and became one of the most famous dogs in the world.

(based on an incident which took place in Chicago)

Prayer
Let us think this morning about the courage of animals. Let us remember Fritz who saved the life of a human being. Let us always look after our pets properly.

Hymn
'All creatures of our God and King' (*Come and Praise* No 7)

Information for the teacher
1   Before coins were invented a man's wealth was measured in terms of the animals he owned, ie sheep, cattle, etc.

2   A man considered to be compassionate and righteous was concerned about 'the life of his beast' – Proverbs 12:10.

The princess and the peacock   *Creatures*

Introduction
Have you ever thought that you would like to be a faster runner; or a better singer; or a terrific footballer; or somebody who *always* got all their maths right? This morning's story is about a peacock who wished he could . . . well, let's wait and see . . . .

Story
Regal was a peacock who lived in the garden of Princess Jasmine. The garden was enormous and Regal strode around it in a very haughty way. The sun shone on his magnificent feathers and all the other creatures thought how handsome he looked.

One day Regal was strutting round the garden when a nightingale flew overhead. As he flew, the nightingale sang a beautiful song.

'Isn't that lovely?' said a squirrel.

'What a delightful song,' said a tiny mouse. 'How lucky we are to have a nightingale to listen to in our garden.'

'That bird has a splendid voice,' croaked the frog on the edge of his pond.

When Regal heard the song, however, he became very annoyed.

'Why haven't I been given a voice as beautiful as that?' he said to himself. 'It's just not fair. Here I am with feathers of the most marvellous colours; I am the most elegant creature in the whole garden – and I can't sing a note. It's just not fair.'

Regal got more and more unhappy and annoyed as the nightingale continued to sing its beautiful song. Finally the peacock came to a decision.

'I'll go and see Princess Jasmine and complain,' thought Regal, 'I'll tell her how unfair it is.'

So, later that day, when the sun was setting and the sky was streaked with pink and purple, and the garden was cool, Regal went to see Princess Jasmine.

'Well, my beautiful bird,' said the princess, 'What can I do for you?'

'I'm not very happy,' said Regal. 'Just listen to my voice. It's shrill and harsh. The nightingale is not like me. He has a lovely voice. All the creatures admire it when he sings. Fancy a beautiful creature like me not having a voice to match my good looks. I think I should have a better voice. Can you do something about getting me one?'

The princess said nothing. She looked carefully over Regal's beautiful feathers; then she looked over his graceful shape; then she looked at the elegant way he stood. She still said nothing – just stared at the complaining peacock.

Finally Regal began to fell uneasy. Then, as the princess continued to stare at him, he began to feel more and more ashamed.

'I've got so much,' he thought, 'and here I am complaining and wanting more.'

Without another word he turned and went back into the garden. He never complained again.

Prayer
Let us think about how important it is for us to make the most of whatever gifts we have been given. Let us not be jealous and envious people who are always wishing we had something else.

Hymn
'God knows me' (*Come and Praise* No 15)

Information for the teacher
1   The peacock is famous for its spectacular plumage, but it is traditionally associated with vanity – 'proud as a peacock'; 'struts like a peacock'; 'vain as a peacock'.

2   The nightingale belongs to the thrush family. Although shy and unremarkable in appearance, it has a lovely song, which can most often be heard at late evening. Both birds feature in many folk tales.

3   Jesus spent much of his time out of doors – as did many of his followers – and references to birds occur in many of his stories, eg Matthew 6:26; 13:4; 23:27; Luke 9:58; 12:6; 12:24; 13:19.

Lady

Introduction

Have you ever wondered what it would be like not to be able to see? Close your eyes tightly. Now imagine that you have to go about all the time with your eyes closed like that.

There are many people in the world who cannot see. Some of them have guide dogs to help them to go shopping and move about outside.

This morning we are going to hear the words of a blind man called Bill Harman. Bill is more than 80 years old and he has not been able to see for a very, very long time. But this doesn't stop him from travelling all over London and it is his guide dog, Lady, who helps him to do this. Lady is a big black German Shepherd Dog. She and Bill go to lots of schools and Bill talks to the children about his life with Lady. He also does lots of work to raise money for the Guide Dogs for the Blind Association.

I am now going to read to you what Bill says about Lady. Close your eyes tightly while you listen and this will help you to imagine what it is like for Bill.

Bill Harman – speaking about Lady

'When we go out, we take each other. I tell her where to go and she follows my directions. A guide dog only obeys orders. It walks along the pavement till it gets to a kerb, then it awaits instructions. It stops at every step down, even if it's a kerb an inch deep. If I want to cross a road I say 'Forward' and then she waits till it's clear and she judges it's safe. If I don't say 'Forward' she just sits there. She only obeys my orders – forward, right, left etc – but once I give that command my life is in her judgement. Once she starts to move, I'm not in charge of my dog, she is in charge of me . . .

Lady and I travel all over on the railway, sometimes changing trains four times. I know all the London tube stops and when the door opens I give the handle a tiny jerk and she's up like a shot, and I say "Out you go darling" and out she goes. On some stations where there is a choice of trains I have to ask, because Lady can do lots of things but she can't read. I don't like travelling on buses because you can never tell when you are at a stop with all the pausing and starting.'

(from *Your obedient servant* by Angela Patmore, Hutchinson, 1984)

Prayer

Let us pray this morning for people who are blind. Let us also pray for those who do all they can to improve a blind person's life.

Hymn

'Lord of all hopefulness' (*Come and Praise* No 52)

Information for the teacher

1   The idea of training dogs as guides for blind people was first taken up in Germany in 1916. Developments also took place in the USA and Morris Frank became the first American guide dog owner in 1928.

     The training of guide dogs in England began in the early 1930s and the first dogs used were Alsatians. The Guide Dogs for the Blind Association was formally created in 1934.

     Today the Guide Dogs for the Blind Association has several training centres and there are over 2 600 guide dog owners in Britain. The Association breeds most of its guide dogs at its own breeding centre near Warwick. Most of them are Labradors (70%) and 70% are bitches.

     It takes from six to eight months to train a guide dog and the average working life of such a dog is eight years.

2   The address of the Guide Dogs for the Blind Association is:

     Alexandra House, 9–11 Park Street, Windsor, Berks. SL4 1JR Tel: Windsor 55711.

3   A most useful reference book is *Working Dogs* by Joan Palmer (Patrick Stephens, 1983).

A special friend

Creatures

Introduction

We all like to think we have a special friend – somebody who is always there when we need them. This morning's story is about a friend, but a very strange one.

     Some years ago there lived in New Zealand a little girl called Jill. Jill was very quiet and shy and she didn't make friends easily. More than anything else she loved swimming. This is how she came to meet her special friend.

Story

Opononi is a village in New Zealand. It is right beside the sea and many of the men who live there are fishermen. One day when the fishing boats came back to the village the fishermen were very excited.

     'Never seen anything like it,' said one.

     'Nor me,' replied another, 'came right up to the boat he did and even let us stroke him.'

     'Then turned over so we could tickle his tummy,' said another fishermen.

'What are you talking about?' asked one of the fishermen's wives. 'Who came right up to the boat? Who did you stroke?'

'It was a dolphin,' said the fishermen all together. 'A great big, friendly dolphin.'

'Good gracious!' gasped one of the wives. Soon lots of other people were saying the same thing!

The next day the friendly dolphin swam up to the fishermen again. A few days later he swam right into the shore and began playing with people who were swimming there. He let them stroke him and even gave children rides. The people called him Opo, after the name of their village, Opononi.

A few days after this Jill Baker was swimming by herself just off the shore of Opononi. Suddenly she was aware of something swimming beside her – it was the dolphin everybody called Opo! Whatever she did in the water, Opo followed, and nuzzled up close to her to be stroked and petted. Jill had never enjoyed anything as much in her whole life before.

The next day Jill went to the beach again. Putting on her costume she went into the water to swim. Within a few minutes she felt Opo beside her again.

'Opo,' she cried, 'you've come to see me again.'

So began an amazing friendship. Whenever Jill was in the water Opo would suddenly appear beside her. He seemed to know when she was going for a swim and would always join her. Soon he began to carry Jill on his back far out to sea, always taking great care of her. All the long hot summer the two friends met and played in the water.

'I can't explain it,' said Jill to anybody who asked her, 'but we're just really good friends!'

Prayer
Let us think this morning about the pleasure which animals, birds and fish can bring us. Let us learn how to protect them and care for them.

Hymn
'All creatures of our God and King' (*Come and Praise* No 7)

Information for the teacher
1   Unusual friendships might be a topic for further exploration here – old and young; like and unlike; child and animal etc.

2   The true story of Opo had a tragic ending in 1956. Flocks of tourists came to the quiet village of Opononi to see the friendly dolphin. There were complaints that the village was becoming spoiled and over-commercialised. Then one day Opo's dead body was found on the rocks. The cause of death was never discovered.

The dolphin was buried with great ceremony and a special service was taken by Maoris. The grave is still carefully tended and remains a tourist attraction. It was said at the time that Opo had been sent to make people of all races believe in the value of friendship and peace.

3   Stories of friendly dophins were common in Greek and Roman times. There were tales of sailors, and particularly children, being saved from drowning by dolphins. Apart from Opo the most famous dolphin of modern times was Pelorous Jack who, for twenty years, followed the ferries back and forth from Nelson to Wellington in New Zealand. A special law was made to protect him and he died of old age in 1912.

4   The dolphin appears frequently in Christian art. In many cases it symbolises 'salvation' – this association often being linked with its strength and speed. In some paintings it can be seen with an anchor or boat; this symbolises the Church being guided to salvation by Christ.

The water carrier   *Creatures*

Introduction
This morning's story is about a donkey. He lives a very long way away in Africa and he has a special job to do. His name is Bo.

Story
'I do like being a nurse, Mum,' said Maureen to her mother, 'but I think I would like to go and work in a part of the world where people most need help.'

'Where do you mean?' asked Maureen's Mum.

'Africa,' replied Maureen. 'When mothers and children are starving they need as much help as they can get. Many need help desperately in Africa.'

So Maureen asked Save the Children if they could help her to find a job in Africa, and before very long she found herself in a small town called Sebba in West Africa. There she met Jenni, another nurse.

'We are certainly needed here,' said Jenni. 'The children are almost always hungry because the harvests are poor.'

'I'm glad we'll be able to help,' replied Maureen, 'but this house we're living in – there's something missing.'

'You mean water! Ahah but you haven't met the other person who lives here, have you?'

Smiling mysteriously, Jenni took Maureen to the back of the house and there, standing in the shade, stood a donkey.

'Meet Bo,' said Jenni.

'But . . . what does he do?' asked Maureen.

'Well you mentioned water, We have to get our water from the village pump every day. The water pots are much too heavy for us to carry. Anyway, it's much too hot to carry the water, and the roads are usually covered in layers of sand. So guess who is the only person who can get our water?'

'Bo.'

'You're right. We just couldn't manage without this lovely old donkey, and by doing what he does he helps us to help all these poor children here.'

'I see what you mean. Bo is very special, isn't he?'

Prayer

Let us remember this morning a lady called Eglantyne Jebb. Many years ago she saw starving children and, by herself, she started collecting money to help them. She was the lady who started the organisation we now know as Save the Children – which helps so many poor and starving children. Let us pray for its continuing good work.

Hymn
'The family of man' (*Come and Praise* No 69)

Information for the teacher
1   By distributing pamphlets asking for help, Eglantyne Jebb raised £400 000 to care for starving Austrian children after the First World War. She continued her efforts, first helping Armenian children, and then the 6 000 000 who were starving in Russia in the early 1920s when the harvest failed. Eglantyne Jebb died in 1920 but the organisation she founded is still flourishing today.

2   Much useful information for assemblies and RE can be obtained from *Satellite*, The Young Save the Children magazine. Georgette Floyd is the editor and the address is:

   Young Save the Children, Grove Lane, London SE5 8RD.

3   The most famous donkey of all is probably the one on which Jesus made his entry into Jerusalem. Two others of note are linked with the saints Anthony and Jerome. Saint Anthony was supposedly trying to convert a man to Christianity when a wild donkey passed by. The man said he could only be convinced if the donkey stopped and knelt – which, to everyone's amazement, it did. The donkey in the St Jerome story was

rather like Bo in this assembly story. It became famous for carrying wood to a monastery.

4   In Jerusalem there is a Biblical zoo which contains as many as possible of the animals mentioned in the Bible.

Be content   *Creatures*

Introduction
This morning's story is about a foolish toad. This toad, whose name was Terence, always wanted to be something else. He wanted to be a *very important person*. This is his story.

Story
'Why can't I be important?' thought Terence the toad to himself.

'I do so want to be a very important person.'

Then he had an idea.

'I know what I'll do,' he thought. 'I'll move away to another part of the wood where nobody knows me and I'll pretend to be . . . a doctor! Everybody thinks doctors are very important.'

So Terence moved to another part of the wood. Then he got himself a long white coat, and a stethoscope, and he perched a pair of spectacles on the end of his nose.

Dressed like this he strolled about the wood, clearing his throat impatiently and saying 'Hmmmmm' out loud every now and again.

'Have you seen who is wandering about the wood at the moment?' said Rabbit one day to Badger.

'I have indeed,' replied Badger. 'It's a doctor isn't it?'

'Marvellous,' said Squirrel. 'A doctor has come to live in our part of the wood.'

'Now we'll all be as healthy as can be,' said Rabbit. 'As a matter of fact I should see the doctor now because I've got this pain in my leg.'

'Why don't we all go to see him?' asked Badger. 'Then he can make sure that we are all fit and healthy.'

'What a brilliant idea,' said Squirrel. 'He walks the same way every morning. We'll wait for him.'

Meanwhile Terence had been enjoying himself enormously. He had noticed the animals looking at him as he strolled importantly through the wood.

'Ah,' he sighed to himself as he pulled on his white coat the next morning. 'What it is to be an important person.'

Soon he was walking along his usual path. He turned a corner, and to his surprise, found a great crowd of animals waiting for him.

'Good morning doctor,' they all cried.

'Oh . . . er . . . good morning,' replied Terence.

Then the questions started. 'I've got this pain . . . what's the matter with that . . . do you know about . . . '

Fortunately for Terence everybody talked at once – so he didn't have to give any answers. He just stood there nodding and saying 'Hmmmm' every now and then. He felt VERY important.

Meanwhile Fox had arrived on the edge of the crowd. Standing at the back he looked and listened for some time. Then, pushing his way to the front, he came face to face with Terence. Looking the toad straight in the eye he said slowly:

'I don't think for a moment you are a doctor. Are you?'

Terence took a deep breath, gasped once or twice, and then looked at the ground. He had been found out.

(adapted from an old Armenian folk tale)

Prayer

Let us pray this morning that we will always be honest and never try to pretend that we can do something if we can't. Let us pray for real doctors and all the work they do in keeping us healthy.

Hymn

'God knows me' (*Come and Praise* No 15)

Information for the teacher

1   This story is about cheating, in that a person pretends to be something that he is not. Many similar stories are to be found in folk tales from all over the world.

2   A possible extension of this 'cheating' theme could involve a different situation – where an agreement is reached and then one of the parties cheats by not honouring it. A good example of a tale on this theme is that of the Pied Piper of Hamelin, in which the townsfolk attempt to go back on their bargain. A beautifully-illustrated book which contains this story is *Fairy Tales*, retold by Bridget Hadaway (Octopus, 1974). The tale is told in full in *The Story of the Pied Piper* by Barbara Ireson, illustrated by Gerald Ross (Faber and Faber, 1961).

Dog hero of the year *Creatures*

Introduction

In the United States of America, every year a dog is chosen as 'Dog hero of the year'. To win this award, a dog has to do something very special.

This morning's story is about Zorro, a German Shepherd Dog, and how he became 'Dog hero of the year'.

Story

Mark looked down at his big strong dog and patted his head.

'You're going to enjoy this, Zorro,' he said. 'We are going for a long walk in the mountains. There will be just the two of us and we'll have a great time.'

Zorro barked and licked his master's hand.

Two hours later Mark and Zorro were climbing the lower slopes of the mountains. Mark had a big pack on his back so that he could use both hands.

'This is hard work,' gasped Mark to Zorro. He was climbing up lots of loose rock and it was very hard for his feet to get a good grip.

'You are better than me,' laughed Mark as Zorro climbed nimbly ahead. Then it happened!

One of Mark's feet slipped on the loose rocks and before he could stop himself he was slipping and sliding down the steep slope. He fell faster and faster, cutting his hands and his head as he did so. Finally in a crash of rocks and loose stones Mark plunged into a river at the bottom of the slope.

Desperately worried about his master Zorro dashed down the slope after him. He whined anxiously as Mark plunged into the water – then the dog noticed that his master was not moving. Splashing into the water Zorro got his teeth round the unconscious Mark's collar and dragged him up the slope to safety. As soon as he let go, however, the weight of the back pack caused his master to slide back down the slope into the water.

Again the brave dog dragged Mark out, again he slid back into the water. After pulling him out for a third time Zorro decided that the only thing to do was to sit on Mark's legs so that he would not slide again.

A few minutes later Mark recovered consciousness. He realised that he was badly hurt.

'Zorro,' he gasped, 'I'm soaking wet so I reckon you must have pulled me out of that water. You've saved my life.'

Zorro gave a bark of joy to hear his master's voice again. Mark stroked him thankfully.

'Now my old friend, we've just got to wait here until a helicopter comes to rescue us,' went on Mark.

Some time later, when Mark and Zorro failed to check in after their mountain trip, the rescue helicopter set out to look for them. They were soon spotted and one of the helicopter crew was lowered by rope to see how badly Mark was hurt.

'We'll need to put you on a stretcher,' said the man to Mark. This was done and the stretcher was winched into the helicopter.

'But my dog – what about poor Zorro?' gasped Mark.

'Don't worry,' said the man from the helicopter, 'another group of rescuers are on their way on foot. They will look after your dog.'

So Zorro sat patiently guarding his master's back pack until the other rescuers arrived and took him back with them.

Once Mark got to hospital he soon got well again, and the story of Zorro's courage was in all the newspapers. Soon after, he was chosen to be Dog Hero of the Year.

Prayer
Let us think this morning about people who spend their holidays walking, climbing or camping. Let us think of those who help them if an accident occurs. Let us not forget that the helpers are often animals as well as people.

Hymn
'We are climbing' (*Come and Praise* No 49)

Information for the teacher
1   Since 1954 the Quaker Oats Company has sponsored the Dog Hero of the Year award in the USA. Zorro won the award in 1975. His courageous acts took place in the Sierra Nevada mountain range, when his master, Mark Cooper, fell an estimated 85 feet, sustaining several injuries.

2   A useful address in connection with this story might be:
      The Outward Bound Trust, Iddesleigh House, Caxton Street, London SW1.

Happy Birthday, Julie   *Special Occasions*

Introduction
Birthdays are very special times. This morning's story is about how a little girl thought she was going to be disappointed one birthday.

Story
Julie pressed her nose on the window as she looked outside. Down below the flat where she and her Mummy and Daddy lived, the buses and cars

moved along like pretty coloured toys. Julie sighed and her breath clouded up the window.

'I wish I could,' she said to herself.

'What, dear?' asked Mummy, who was sitting on the couch knitting.

'Oh nothing Mummy,' answered Julie. She knew that although it was her birthday next week it was no good asking for what she really wanted. She liked this bright new flat but, she had heard Daddy reading a letter out to Mummy when they first moved in.

'It says here,' Dad had said, 'no animals allowed.' Julie had had to go into her bedroom when she heard this. She didn't want Mummy and Daddy to see how sad that news made her feel. More than anything she had wanted a pet for her birthday.

'Look Julie, there's Daddy.'

Mummy had put away her knitting and was standing at the window too. As she pointed down, Julie saw Daddy walking along the street towards the block of flats.

'He's carrying something,' said Julie.

'Hmmmm,' answered Mummy. 'Hmmmm.'

Soon Daddy was home. He put the big brown parcel in the hall. Then they all had tea.

'Can I watch television, Mummy?' asked Julie when they had finished tea. To her surprise Mummy said, 'Not tonight Julie. Daddy's going to be busy. Why don't you draw instead?'

As Julie got out her crayons and drawing paper Daddy unwrapped the parcel. There were some big pieces of glass inside it. Then Daddy plugged in his electric drill and began to make some holes in the wall. For a long time he worked hard. He measured and drilled and cut the glass with a special knife.

'What are you making, Dad?' asked Julie.

Daddy didn't answer but when he looked at Julie he gave a great big wink.

. . . .

Soon it was Julie's birthday. She woke up very early and switched on the light. Mummy had put all her cards and presents beside her bed. She opened the cards first. There was one from Mummy, one from Gran and Grandad, one from Uncle Bob and Auntie Mary and lots more. Then she began to open her presents.

When she had opened all her cards and presents Julie sat looking at the pile of books and games and toys, and suddenly she thought of something! There was no card or present from Dad.

She felt very sad, but then she thought how busy Dad had been. Perhaps he had forgotten and would be getting something today. She still felt sad though.

'Breakfast Julie.' Mummy's voice came from the other room. Putting on her dressing gown Julie got up and went into the living room.

As soon as she got through the door she stopped. Her eyes opened wide with surprise and delight. There, fixed to the wall, was a fish tank, and in it were the most beautiful little fish you have ever seen. Standing beside the tank was a birthday card and even from where she was Julie could read the writing on it. It said: 'Happy Birthday from Dad'.

Prayer
Let us pray that we might be as thoughtful as Julie's Dad when it is the birthday of someone we know. Let us give thanks for the love and warmth of a family and friend and let us pray for all those unfortunate people who are lonely.

Hymn
'The King of Love' (*Come and Praise* No 54)

Help   *Special Occasions*

Introduction
Can you think of one of the most special days in your life? ('Birthday' is the answer being sought here!)

One of the exciting things about birthdays is that cards often come through the post for us. This morning's story is about a boy who never got any letters or cards – until one very special day . . .

Story
The young Greek boy was desperate. He was working in a shop in a big city and sending money home to help his family who were very poor. He was lonely and unhappy and he was underpaid by his master.

'What can I do?' he thought to himself. 'My family need more money and so do I. I can't even afford a pair of shoes.'

Each day the boy saw a pile of letters arrive for the owner of the shop where he worked. Each night he was given a pile of letters to post.

'If only I had somebody to write to,' the boy thought. 'Then perhaps they could help me or tell me what to do.'

He couldn't write to his family because none of them could read.

Then one day the boy had an idea. He wrote a letter. In it he explained how desperate he was and asked for help. Then he put the letter in an envelope and addressed it to: 'Jesus'

That night the boy took his own letter along with all the others he was given to post. On his way to the post office he was stopped by another shopkeeper who always felt sorry for him.

'Go on,' said the shopkeeper, 'it's a long way to the post office. I'll take your letters. You get off home early for a change.'

The shopkeeper took all the letters, but as he was posting them he noticed the one addressed to Jesus. He was so astonished that he opened it there and then. A few days later the boy got a letter addressed to him. In it was some money.

From this point onwards the boy did as much as he could to help other people. He spent the rest of his life helping others, and by the time he died he had become famous.

Prayer

This morning's story is a reminder that all of us need help at some time. The boy in the story was so lonely that he felt only Jesus could help him – and in a mysterious way his letter to Jesus brought help.

Let us think this morning of those poor and lonely people who are desperate for help right now, even as we pray here. Let us pray that help may be given to them.

Hymn

'Lost and Found' (*Come and Praise* No 57)

Information for the teacher

1   The name of the boy in the story was Anastassios. Despite his lack of education he eventually became a teacher, a monk, a bishop and Dean of a Theological College. After his death in 1920 he was canonized by the Greek Orthodox Church under the name of St Nectarios.

2   A possible discussion point with regard to this assembly is that 'taking action' sometimes yields unexpected results, but inaction in such a situation cannot help. A possible Bible reference in this connection could be: Judges: 11–16.

3   Letters (in the context of correspondence) feature prominently throughout the Bible. Perhaps with children of this age and in the context of this story some comment on the importance of a 'scribe' in Biblical times might be useful. The scribe was a most important person in towns and villages. People who could not read or write would hire the scribe to write letters or draw up documents.

When I learned to whistle   *Special Occasions*

Introduction
There are some special occasions which we never forget. Christmas is one, and our birthday is another. Guy Fawkes' Night is an exciting time too.

But there are other kinds of special occasions too – when we first learn to ride a bike, or swim, or skip, or play the recorder.

When we do something like this it is nice to hear somebody say: 'Well done – that's good!'

This morning we are going to listen to a poem about a little boy who did something for the first time.

When I learned to whistle

I remember the day when I learned to whistle,
It was Spring and new sounds were all around.
I was five or six and my front teeth were missing,
But I blew until my cheeks stuck out.

I remember walking up and down the block,
Trying to impress those that heard me
With the tunes and sounds that came from my mouth,
For I sounded much better than the birds in the trees.

I remember being hurt, for nobody seemed to care,
And then I met an old man who stopped and smiled,
He too blew until his cheeks stuck out.
He sounded just like me, for his front teeth were missing.

Gordon Lea

Prayer
Let us pray this morning for two things. Let us pray that we might always have help and encouragement to learn new skills.

Next, let us pray that, having learned to do something new, we try to do it as well as we can from then onwards.

Hymn
'Fill your heart with joy and gladness' (*Come and Praise* No 9)

Information for the teacher
Perhaps a useful follow-up here would be to consider that when we learn to do something we should then try to do it as well as we can. Sometimes, and

in certain circumstances, failure to do this can have unpleasant results. A rather dramatic reference to illustrate this could be the story of the boy whose carelessness whilst shoeing Richard III's horse ultimately caused his master's death:

> For want of a nail a shoe was lost
> For want of a shoe a horse was lost
> For want of a horse a rider was lost
> For want of a rider a battle was lost
> For want of a battle a kingdom was lost
> And all for the want of a horseshoe nail.

Benjamin Franklin

The sausage and his friends

Special Occasions

Introduction

Once upon a time there was a little house in a wood. In this house lived – a sausage, a bird and a mouse. This is their story.

Story

Sam Sausage, Belinda Bird and Michael Mouse all lived together in a neat little house in the woods. They were very happy and each of them did a special job.

Every day Belinda flew into the woods and brought back firewood. Then she got food for tea. When this arrived Michael laid a fire, filled a cooking pot full of water and set the table ready for their meal. When this had been done Sam did the cooking.

'Hi diddle diddle,' sang Sam one day as he was cooking. Then he noticed someone looking in through the window. It was a gang of chips!

'What *are* you doing?' asked the leader of the chips.

'I'm cooking for my friends Belinda and Michael,' said Sam.

'Cooking! Cooking! Who ever heard of a sausage staying at home and cooking? You should be out roaming the woods with a gang of chips.'

With a burst of laughter the chips went on their way. When they had gone Sam called Belinda and Michael and they had their tea. But Sam was thinking nasty thoughts!

'Why should I cook for these two?' he thought. 'I could be having fun in the woods with a gang of chips. Tomorrow I'm going to leave home.'

'Lovely meal Sam,' said Belinda when they had finished eating.

'Smashing,' agreed Michael.

But Sam just grunted.

The next day Belinda collected the firewood and food as usual. Michael got the fire going, put the cooking pot on and laid the table.

'Sam,' he cried. 'Time to make the tea.'

'I can't find him,' said Belinda. 'I think he's gone out.'

Sam had gone out. He soon found one of the gangs of chips who roamed the wood.

'Hi diddle hi,' he sang as he crashed through the woods with them. 'This is the life.'

All day they chased through the woods, and as they did so Sam got hungrier and hungrier.

'Hey, you chips,' he said. 'When do we eat?'

'Oh we just eat any old thing we can,' said one of the chips. 'After all we're just little chips, we don't need much to keep us going.'

'But . . . I'm a big sausage . . . I need my food,' groaned Sam.

'Ha, ha, ha,' laughed the chips. 'Hard luck.'

And so Sam got hungrier and tireder and more miserable. What's more, he began to think of Belinda and Michael.

'Oh dear,' he thought. 'They won't be able to do the cooking. They'll be so miserable.'

So, when it was dark, he left the noisy chips and made the long journey back to the little house in the woods. When he saw the light shining out through its window he thought he had never felt so happy.

Opening the door he went in. Belinda and Michael were sitting by the fire. The big pot of water was boiling away – but there were no lovely cooking smells.

'Belinda, Michael,' said Sam, 'I'm so sorry, you must be starving.'

'Well . . . ' said Michael, 'a bit peckish . . . yes.'

'But,' said Belinda, 'we knew you wouldn't let us down, Sam.'

Sam felt very happy to be home.

Prayer

Let us pray that we never let anybody down. Let us hope that we can always be the sort of person other people can rely on and trust.

Hymn

'The family of man' (*Come and Praise* No 69)

Information for the teacher

1 Two interesting sayings in connection with this assembly might be:

'He who does not help to turn the rolling wheels of this great world lives a lost life.' (Hindu saying)

'A man should treat all the creatures in the world as he himself would like to be treated.' (Jain saying)

2 In nomadic society neighbourliness and sharing tasks and joys were obviously very important – consequently there are many appropriate references in the Bible. Two which could be used are in Luke 15: 6 and 9.

Looking after the baby
Special Occasions

Introduction

Whenever a new baby is born it is a very special time. Those of you who have younger brothers or sisters will know all about this. Now babies need a lot of looking after. They have to be fed at special times and they need lots of sleep. It is a tiring, but very exciting time for mothers.

This morning's story is a very, very old one. It is about a new baby whose mother lived in very different times from today.

Story

'Mum,' said Miriam, 'have you heard the terrible news?'

'Yes,' said Miriam's mother, wiping away a tear.

'What are we going to do with the baby?' Miriam asked.

Miriam and her mother lived in a far off land called Egypt. Now the King of Egypt at that time was a very cruel man. He knew that two kinds of people lived in Egypt – there were the Egyptians, and there were the Israelites.

'I don't want any more Israelites in our country,' he said one day. 'I just want Egyptians. To make sure about this, I want all Israelite baby boys killed at once.'

Now Miriam and her mother were Israelites. They knew their baby was to be killed. What were they to do?

'There is only one thing for it,' said Miriam's mother, and she told of her plan.

The next day Miriam crept down to the river. In her arms she carried a cradle and in the cradle was her baby brother.

Carefully she crept through the bulrushes on the river bank and then put the cradle in the river. It floated gently round. Miriam hid in the bulrushes and waited. Some time later she heard the sound of voices. Miriam saw that it was the King of Egypt's daughter taking her morning walk with some servants.

'Your highness – look!' cried one of the servants, pointing to the cradle in the water.

'It's a baby,' gasped the princess. One of the servants pulled the cradle to the river bank. Carefully the princess took the baby from the cradle and held him in her arms.

'What a lovely child,' she said as the tiny baby smiled at her. 'He must be an Israelite – if only I had somebody to look after him I would keep him and see that he is safe.'

As soon as the princess said this, Miriam pushed her way through the bulrushes and bowed low before the princess.

'Your highness', she said. 'I know of somebody who will look after the baby for you. I can bring her for you at once.'

'Is that so, my child?' said the princess. 'Then bring her immediately.'

Miriam raced away to where her mother was waiting. Within a few minutes they were back and standing in front of the princess.

'Ah,' said the princess. 'I want you to look after this baby for me. See that he comes to no harm and has everything he needs. I am going to call him Moses.'

Miriam and her mother were filled with joy. They had saved their baby – and they were gong to look after him!

Prayer

This morning's story tells us of a cruel man who wanted to harm children. Let us bow our heads and listen to the following words:

'Hurt no living thing –
Ladybird nor butterfly
Nor moth with dusty wing,
Nor cricket chirping cheerily,
Nor grasshopper, so light of leap,
  Nor dancing gnat,
  Nor beetle fat,
Nor harmless worms that creep.'

Christina Rossetti

Hymn

'Lost and found' (*Come and Praise* No 57)

Information for the teacher

1   This story, and the background to it, can be found in Exodus, Chapters 1 and 2. A beautifully illustrated version of it, which is suitable for young children, is contained in '*The Princess and the Baby*' Book 9 of the Lion Story Bible Series.

2   This story can be linked with another example of a mother's initiative which is shown in '*Mother*' on page 115 of this book.

Harvest festival   *Special Occasions*

Introduction

Harvest Festival is a special time in school. We bring along apples, oranges, cucumbers, tins of fruit, packets of biscuits and lots of other food. When we have put these things where everybody can see them we thank God for all the good things in the world. After the Harvest Festival service we give the food away to people who need it; or we sell it and send the money to other countries where people are starving.

It is hard to imagine that Harvest Festival has anything to do with smugglers – but this morning's story will tell you how it has. The story starts a long time ago in a part of England called Cornwall.

Story

Robert Hawker was worried. He had been made vicar of a little village called Morwenstow in Cornwall and he was worried about the people who lived there.

'They are doing such awful things,' he said to his wife. 'I've seen them lighting fires on the rocks at night. The ships at sea think that the light from the fires is guiding them on a safe course, but really it is guiding them onto the rocks. Then, when the ships hit the rocks and sink, the village people steal all the goods from the wreck.'

'That's terrible,' said Mrs Hawker.

'And there's more,' went on the Vicar, 'On those little beaches nobody visits, smugglers bring goods ashore in the dead of night.'

'What are you going to do about it?' asked Mrs Hawker.

'Well, one thing I'm going to do,' replied the Vicar, 'is to try and make our church a lovely place to come to. Then when the villagers come to it I hope we'll be able to persuade them to stop doing these dreadful deeds.'

So Robert Hawker started on his work. People soon got to know that he was a very kind man who would always give help. Then the villagers began to talk about some of the things that went on in his church.

'Never seen anything like it,' said one of them on a late September day.

'Really?'

'No, he asked everybody to bring some sort of food to church. Well, we had potatoes, cabbages, carrots, apples, pears, loaves of bread – and then everything was made up into a lovely display. After that we sang hymns and gave thanks for the food.'

'But what is he going to do with the food now?'

'Oh, he is going to take it to the poor and sick people who don't get enough.'

'That's a good idea.'

'It certainly is – and we had a marvellous time in the church. A Harvest Festival, Mr Hawker called it.'

So the villagers of Morwenstow all started to go to Robert Hawker's church. Other people who lived in nearby villages heard about what was happening and they came too.

Robert was Vicar of Morwenstow for 41 years. During that time most of the villagers gave up wrecking ships and smuggling. Robert helped them to look at, and think about, the beautiful countryside and how they might help each other instead of killing and robbing poor sailors. We still remember Robert Hawker as the man who started Harvest Festival services.

Prayer
Let us thank God for the sun and the rain which make our crops grow. Let us give thanks for the food we have to eat, and let us pray that those who don't have enough can be helped.

Hymn
'Thank you Lord' (*Come and Praise* No 32)

Information for the teacher
1   Stories of farming and harvesting are prolific in the Bible. Dwellers in Palestine are thought to have farmed for over 10 000 years. In 1908 a limestone plaque dating from 950 BC was discovered, it contained a farmer's programme: olive harvest, grain planting, hoeing, barley harvest, festivity, vine tending, summer fruit. Useful Bible references: Isaiah 28: 23–29; Mark 4: 26–32; Luke 22:31.

2   The story of Ruth and Boaz (Ruth: 1–4) makes a change from the parable of the sower and the seed for any teachers who wish to use a Bible story in this context.

3 Organisations such as Save the Children, Oxfam and Christian Aid can provide information about farming in the Third World, and how aid programmes help with this. An interesting alternative might be to discuss the 'fish harvest' and useful material can be obtained from:
Fish Education Service, 30 Farringdon Street, London EC4

4 Useful sources of reference for teachers wishing to concentrate on farming in Britain are:
The Association of Agriculture, Victoria Chambers, 16/20 Strutton Ground, London SW1
Farming Today, the BBC's agricultural broadcast.

Mother

Special Occasions

Introduction

Mothers are *very* special people. We often hear stories about mothers doing brave things to protect their children.

This morning's story is about how a mother saved her little boy's life.

Story

Rachid was four years old and he was always looking for adventures.

'I wonder what's going on over there?' he thought one day when he saw a crowd of people near a quarry where he lived.

'Look!' he cried out loud, 'a firework.'

On Guy Fawkes Night, the week before, Rachid had seen his dad light lots of fireworks. Now he could see what looked just like a firework . . . a long thing which was burning at one end. He pushed through a crowd of people and ducked under a rope to get a better look.

As he did so there was a shout of 'Come back little boy . . . hey . . . come back.'

Rachid was so interested in the firework that he didn't even hear.

Now I expect you have guessed that what Rachid saw was not a firework at all. Some workmen were cutting rock from the quarry. To do this they drilled a hole in the rock and filled it with gunpowder. They attached a fuse to the gunpowder and then, when everything was ready, they lit the fuse.

What Rachid thought was a firework was the fuse leading to the gunpowder. The rope he climbed under showed that it wasn't safe to go any nearer the fuse. Rachid was now much too close to it. Any minute the gunpowder would explode and hundreds of tons of rocks would be blown into the air – and they might land on top of Rachid!

'Come back little boy!'

'It's dangerous, come back.'

'Hey, little lad – get back!'

Suddenly everybody in the crowd was shouting to Rachid to come back. But nobody was brave enough to run past the rope and get him because they knew the explosion could take place any second.

Rachid stood and watched the twinkling fire on the end of the fuse. He heard all the noise but he didn't pay any attention to it. Then . . .

'Rachid!'

Rachid turned. That was his mother's voice. There she was. She had stepped over the rope and was kneeling down with her arms open wide.

'Mum', he shouted and ran towards her. Throwing himself into her arms he was just pressing his face to hers when there was a tremendous '*Bang*' and rocks hurtled down to where Rachid had been standing.

His mother pushed the hair back out of his eyes. She had known that she hadn't time to run after him so she had done the only thing a mother could do when her child was in danger – and Rachid had seen her open arms in time.

Prayer
Let us pray for all those who care for us and keep us safe from harm. Let us pray for mothers, fathers and children everywhere.

Hymn
'He's got the whole world' (*Come and Praise* No 17)

Information for the teacher
1   A useful and detailed definition of 'love' can be found in 1 Corinthians 13: 4–7.

2   The following is an appropriate poem to use with this story:

Boy

Mum'll be coming home today.
It's three weeks she's been away.
When Dad's alone all we eat
is cold meat
which I don't like
and he burns the toast I want just-brown
and I hate taking the ash can down.

He's mended the door
from the little fight
on Thursday night
so it doesn't show
and we can have grilled tomatoes
Spanish onions and roast potatoes
and will you sing me 'I'll never more roam'
when I'm in bed, when you've come home.

Michael Rosen

One more for the family
Special Occasions

Introduction
If you have a dog or a cat you will know how important it is to keep them
indoors on Fireworks Night, 5 November. This is because they could so easily
be frightened by the bangs and get hurt trying to run away.

This morning's story is about what happened one Fireworks Night to an
old lady, a dog and a cat.

Story
Mrs Vickery lived with Roger in a small cottage beside a school playing field.
Mrs Vickery was an old lady with bright rosy cheeks and grey hair which
was twisted into a bun at the back of her head. Roger was an Old English
sheepdog, friendly and floppy and good natured. At least, he *was* good
natured, until a certain Fireworks Night.

'You'll have to stay in tonight, Roger,' said Mrs Vickery. 'They're having
a big bonfire out on the field. There'll be lots of fireworks and bangs and
noise – no place for a dog to be.'

Roger gave a snuffle. He didn't quite understand all of what was being
said but he knew what 'staying in' meant – a nice cosy fire. Who wanted to
go out anyway!

Soon after dark Mrs Vickery gave Roger some of his favourite dog food.
After eating it he settled down in his most comfortable spot in front of the
fire – one eye open, one eye closed.

He watched his mistress go to the window and look out.

'There they go,' she said. 'Its a very big fire this year and I
suppose . . . what's that?'

Mrs Vickery said the last two words in such a different way that Roger opened both eyes immediately. Next thing he knew his mistress was hurrying to the door and going outside.

'Hmmm,' thought Roger. 'What can she be doing? It's cold with that door open.'

Within a couple of minutes Mrs Vickery was back – and Roger could not believe his eyes! She was carrying a *cat*!

Now Roger had both eyes wide open. To let his mistress know what he thought about things he let out a low growl.

'Quiet Roger,' said Mrs Vickery. 'This poor little cat was out there in all that noise and danger. She's terrified; I think she's a stray.'

Roger growled.

What happened next made him even more angry. First his mistress gave the cat some milk and then she went and got the basket Roger had used when he was a puppy. Plumping a cushion in this she put it beside the fire and began to make ridiculous noises.

'Kitty-kitty-kitty. Kitty-kitty-kitty. Here kitty.'

This time Roger not only growled, he got up and turned his back on Mrs Vickery and the cat.

Slowly time passed. Every time there was a bang outside the frightened cat gave a tiny miaow and Mrs Vickery stroked it and made her ridiculous noises again.

Roger sulked. He wouldn't drink his water, he kept his eyes shut when Mrs Vikery stroked him and every now and then he growled – just to let *everybody* know how he felt. To bring a cat into *his* house indeed, and to put it in *his* old basket. How could she do anything so dreadful?

The stray cat stayed the next day . . . and the next . . . and the next. Mrs Vickery called it Nibbles and she even gave it drinks in one of Roger's old bowls. Roger was furious and he sulked even more.

Then one night Mrs Vickery put a bowl of Roger's favourite dog food out for him. Roger's nose twitched at the lovely smell. He couldn't resist it any more. As he bent to eat it Mrs Vickery stroked his back.

'Oh Roger,' she said. 'You'll always be my own special Roger you know – but there is room for us to share our house with another friend.'

As she spoke a small whiskery face suddenly appeared bside Roger's and nuzzled him. 'It's that cat . . . ' thought Roger, starting to get angry again. But the friendly rubbing against him, his mistress's calm voice and the warm fire . . . all of these things made him think how silly it was to get angry and sulky. Suddenly Roger felt as happy as he had done before Nibbles came – no that's not quite true – he felt happier!

Prayer
Let us think this morning about animals in danger. As we do so let us

remember a Hindu saying: 'You can always talk to the Lord. He will always hear you because he can even hear the footsteps of an ant.'

Hymn
'From the darkness came light' (*Come and Praise* No 29)

Information for the teacher
1 Dogs traditionally symbolise watchfulness and fidelity. Cats, however, have more sinister associations in folklore, with witchcraft and black magic. An exception is the legend of the 'cat of the Madonna', where the story goes that a cat gave birth to a litter of kittens in the stable at the same time as Jesus was born.

2 Recordings of dramatic music can help children appreciate how easy it is for animals to become frightened on 5 November. Some good examples are: *Ritual Fire Dance* by Falla; *Music for the Royal Fireworks* by Handel; and the *Firebird Suite* by Stravinsky.

3 An amusing and significant story about the dangers of fireworks relates how the Chinese were the first to invent and use rockets 1000 years ago. One day an important Chinaman decided to launch a kite by propelling it with rockets. Unfortunately, he forgot to let go – and disappeared into the sky himself!

Diwali
Special Occasions

Introduction
What do you think is the most exciting time of the year? (Wait for the answer – Christmas!) At Christmas people often put coloured lights on their Christmas trees and decorate their houses. Hindu boys and girls also celebrate a very exciting time by decorating their houses with lots of lights. This special occasion is called *Diwali* or the 'Festival of Lights'.

At Diwali everybody thinks of a famous king called Rama. This morning's story is about him, and it took place a long, long time ago in a country called India.

Story
A long, long time ago there lived a king in India. One day he called his chief ministers together.

'I am getting too old to be your king,' he said, 'so I am going to make one of my sons king in my place. Prince Rama is the son I have chosen.'

The ministers were delighted and so was nearly everybody else in the kingdom when they heard the news. They all liked the old king but if he had to give up the throne then they were pleased Prince Rama would be the next king. Prince Rama was kind and fair and brave, and all the people in the kingdom knew this.

'He'll make a wonderful king,' they all said to each other.

But there was one person who was not happy. This was one of the king's wives, called Kaikeyi. She wanted her son, Bharata, to be king. So she went to see the old king.

'Your majesty,' she said. 'You remember when we were out hunting and I used my bow and arrow to shoot a tiger which attacked you?'

'I do remember,' said the king. 'You saved my life.'

'Do you also remember,' went on Kaikeyi, 'that you promised me I could have two wishes for saving your life.'

'Yes,' said the king.

'Well, I want to claim my two wishes now,' said Kaikeyi. 'I want my son Bharata to be king instead of Rama, and I want Rama to be sent away from here for fourteen years.'

The old king looked sad and worried, but he had to keep his promise.

'Very well,' he said slowly.

So Bharata became king and Rama was sent away into the forests. The old king was so sorry about this that he died very quickly.

Bharata too was very unhappy. He knew Rama would be a better king and he was angry at his mother for the way she had behaved. When the old king died he went to see Rama in the forests.

'Listen my brother,' he said, 'our father has died. Please come back and be king now.'

'I can't do that, said Rama. 'I was sent away for fourteen years so I must stay away until that time is passed.'

'I will return for you then,' said Bharata and he went back to the palace. When he got there he put a pair of Rama's golden sandals on the king's throne.

'They will stay there until Rama has returned to be king,' he said.

So the golden sandals stayed on the throne for fourteen years. When this time had passed Bharata led his people into the town. They took with them hundreds and hundreds of lamps which made a great light. Far away in the forests, Rama saw the light, and it guided him back to the palace. There was great rejoicing when Rama took his sandals off the throne and sat on it. He was king at last.

Prayer
'Lead us from the unreal to the real,
 Lead us from darkness to light.'

(Hindu scriptures)

Hymn
'From the darkness came light' (*Come and Praise* No 29)

Information for the teacher
1   Diwali, the great Hindu Festival of Lights, could quite easily be linked
    with Christmas in a 'Light' theme. During his 14 years in exile Rama
    had to rescue his wife Sita from the demon king Ravanna, so the
    celebrations on his return were particularly joyful. Thousands of clay
    lamps lit his way back to the throne.

2   Diwali falls in late October/early November and can also be linked with
    the Jewish Festival of Lights.

3   A useful address is:
    Shap Working Party on World Religions, 7 Alderbrooke Road, Solihull,
    West Midlands B91 1NH

4   Recorded music to 'set the scene' for this story can be found on *Music
    of India*, Ravi Shankar and Akbar Khan, (EMI ALP 2304).

Out of the bad came good   *Special Occasions*

Introduction
Christmas is an exciting time which we all enjoy. Putting up decorations,
giving and getting presents, cosy homes, twinkling lights . . . Ah, twinkling
lights. This is a true story about twinkling lights at Christmas. It happened
in a school just like the one you are in now . . .

Story
Dewhurst School is just outside London and the children who go to it are
aged between 5 and 11. Every year these children feel extra specially lucky
at Christmas time. This is because in a garden in the middle of the school

stands a huge Christmas tree. It is taller than three men and every year in December, the caretaker covers it with sparkling lights and then switches them on. The lovely lights shine through dull December afternoons and remind everybody that the most exciting season of the year is near.

'It's special to us, that tree,' said Patricia to her friend one afternoon when they were getting ready to go home. 'You can't even see it from outside the school – so aren't we lucky!'

But one morning . . .

'I've got some bad news,' said the caretaker to the headmaster when he arrived at school. 'Come and see.'

The two men went to the garden and the caretaker pointed. The lights from the Christmas tree were gone!

Soon the police had been informed. They found out that somebody had climbed over the school roof during the night, pulled all the lights off the tree and taken them away. The policeman was shocked.

'That's the meanest crime I've heard of this year,' he said. 'Do you mind if I tell the local papers about it?'

'I think that's a very good idea,' said the headmaster. 'It might help to stop any more thefts like this.'

Within a few days the local paper had a front page story about the missing lights. 'Meanest crime of the year,' – it said.

Then amazing things began to happen. A Christmas card arrived at the school with £2 in the envelope. It came from an old lady who wanted to help buy some more lights. Parents of children at the school sent in some more money, and one kind lady arrived at school with another box of outdoor tree lights. Within days the tree was alive with twinkling lights again – and there was enough money left over to go towards buying another, smaller treee to stand in the school entrance.

Now when people think of the Christmas when the lights disappeared they think about all the good things which happened afterwards.

Prayer

Let us think this morning about all the things around us which remind us of Christmas. Let us think about those sad people who steal at this time of the year. Let us hope that they too can have kind families and friends so that they are happier and are not tempted to do hurtful things.

Hymn

'From the darkness came light' (*Come and Praise* No 29)

Information for the teacher

1   The use of lights in festivals is common throughout the world. Two to

which reference might be made here are the Jewish Festival of Lights – Hanukkah; and the Hindu celebration of Diwali.

2   Light often symbolises Good and Darkness – Evil.

3   Light features frequently in the Bible: God's word was a light to the path of the faithful (Ps. 119:105); John the Baptist said Jesus' coming would be a light to light every man (John 1:4).

A carol for Christmas   *Special Occasions*

Introduction
(It would be helpful to sing or listen to 'Silent Night' at the start of this assembly.)

At Christmas we sing special songs called carols. One of the most lovely of these is 'Silent Night'. This morning's story is about the men who wrote 'Silent Night'. They lived a long time ago in a village high in the mountain snows of Austria. Joseph was a priest and Franz played the organ in the village church.

Story
It was Christmas Eve. The snow lay thickly on the tiny village of Oberndorf. Joseph Mohr, the village priest, was looking forward to the Christmas Eve carol service.

'Franz,' he said to the organist, Franz Gruber, 'let's go to the church and practise the carols for tonight.'

The two went into the church. The organ was an old-fashioned one and air had to be pumped into it before it would work.

'I'll play first while you pump the organ,' said Joseph.

'Just as you like,' replied Franz, and he went behind the organ and started pumping the handle.

'Come on, come on,' shouted Joseph. 'Pump some air in.'

'I am,' shouted Franz crossly.

The two men then realised that something was wrong. The organ would not play. When they looked into the back of the organ they got a terrible shock. There was a great big hole in the bellows which pumped in the air. The hole had been eaten by . . . a mouse!

'Would you believe it?' gasped Franz. 'A mouse has put the organ out of action.'

'It's not funny,' replied Joseph. 'This is the most important night of the whole year and we have no organ.'

'Not a chance of getting it repaired by tonight either,' said Franz.

'Everybody will be so disappointed, no organ to play those lovely carols,' went on Joseph.

'Listen Joseph,' said Franz, after a pause. 'People won't be so disappointed if you and I get together and make a brand new carol that nobody has ever heard before.'

'Why, yes,' agreed Joseph, 'especially if we can manage to make it a good one . . . '

So the two men went back to Joseph's house.

'Now Franz,' said Joseph, 'you're the best organist around these parts so you write the music, and I'll try and work out some words.'

'Right Joseph – but I've got a good idea for the title. Thanks to that mouse it was almost a 'silent night' here, so why don't we call it that?'

'Brilliant idea!' said Joseph. 'Silent Night. Now let's see . . . '

The two men worked hard and quickly for there was not much time.

At midnight the church bell rang out over the still, snowy village night. Carrying lights and bundled in their warmest clothes the villagers walked through the snow to the church. When they were all inside, Joseph spoke.

'My friends,' he said. 'Franz, our organist, and I have been working on a new carol. We have tried to make the words and music remind us not only of that night long ago in Bethlehem, but also of our good fortune in living in this beautiful part of Austria.'

Franz then began to play 'Silent Night' on his guitar, while Joseph sang the words. Soon all the villagers were joining in. They thought they had just heard one of the loveliest of all carols. I am sure you will agree!

Prayer
Silent night, holy night,
All is calm, all is bright,
Round yon Virgin mother and child.
Holy infant, so tender and mild,
Sleep in heavenly peace,
Sleep in heavenly peace.

Hymn
'Go tell it on the mountain' (*Come and Praise* No 24)

Information for the teacher
The original performance of 'Silent Night' was on Christmas Eve 1818 in the village of Oberndorf in Austria. When the organ was repaired the organist

played 'Silent Night' to test it. The organ repairer was so impressed with this music that he asked for a copy and took it to his home town where it was added to the works performed by the choir there. Thus the carol began to spread. Although there are no statistics to prove it, this is probably one of the most frequently sung carols, all over the world.

The train journey   *Special Occasions*

Introduction
Sometimes at school we have a very special day – we go out on a trip somewhere. This morning's story is about a trip on a very special train called the Orient Express.

Story
'Look at that snow,' said John.

'I've never seen such big flakes before,' replied Julie as she watched the swirling white mass outside the train window.

'You can't see anything but snow,' went on John, 'and . . . do you know something . . . I think the train is going slower.'

'Its not going slower . . . it's stopping,' said Julie.

The train came to a complete stop. There was silence in the compartment and now that there was no movement the snowflakes began to stick to the windows, making a thick, white curtain. Then the door to the compartment opened and the man in charge of the passengers, Pierre, poked his head inside.

'We're stuck, I'm afraid,' he said. 'We're caught in a snowdrift and the train can't move. I think it would be a good idea if everybody got together in one compartment.'

So John and Julie joined all the other passengers. Things soon began to get worse. The snow just would not stop; it got higher and higher and higher – until it was right over the roof of the train. There was no longer any heat on the train and everybody was freezing cold. To add to this they were all hungry and there was hardly any food left.

'We've got to do something,' said John, after they had been stuck for two days.

'Yes, but what?' asked Pierre.

'Let's get all the shovels that are on the train and try and dig our way out.'

'A good idea,' replied Pierre, 'and for those who don't have shovels a piece of wood is better than nothing.'

So all the men on the train got out and began to dig. For hour after hour they worked, making a long tunnel.

'That's not bad,' said one of the diggers, looking back at the tunnel.

'No it's . . . '

Suddenly there was a cracking noise, and the tunnel fell in! Desperately the men set to work again. This time they pulled wood off the train to support the sides of the new tunnel. Finally after digging for two days and nights they burst through into the open air.

'Look, look down there!' cried Pierre, 'A village.'

The men struggled through the thick snow to the village. There they got food and guns. Then they started back to the women who were left on the train. As they got nearer to it they could hear the sound of snarling wolves! The wolves were starving in the snow. They had begun to attack the train in the hope of finding food. A few shots from the guns soon drove them off.

'It's all right,' said John to Julie, when he was back on the train and they had something to eat. 'They're sending a snow plough down the track to get us free.'

Soon they could hear the noise of the snow plough in the distance. In just a few hours the train was freed and could start on its way again. It had been trapped for nearly a week and if the men on it hadn't worked as a team and helped each other it might not have been rescued in time to save their lives.

Prayer
Let us bow our heads this morning and think about working, and playing, together. Let us try to avoid arguments and unkind words, and let us remember to work as a team to get things done.

Hymn
'Lost and found' (*Come and Praise* No 57)

Information for the teacher
This incident took place in January, 1929. The Orient Express was en route from Paris to Istanbul when it ran into a huge snowstorm while crossing the border from Bulgaria to Turkey.

The snowflakes were described by the passengers as being 'as big as hands' and the train was buried 50 miles from its destination. There were 20 passengers on board, and when the train finally pulled into Istanbul it was over a week late.

Carols by candelight

Special Occasions

Introduction

When we think of Christmas in Britain we remember dark nights, cold winds and warm, cosy houses. For people who live in other parts of the world, however, Christmas Day is often one of the hottest of the year. This morning's story is a true one, and it comes from Australia.

Story

Myra looked out of the window at the hot, bright sunshine and she sighed.

'It shouldn't be like this at Christmas,' she thought. 'It never was back at home. Then we had frost and snow and ice – that's *real* Christmas weather.'

Myra lived in Australia but she had grown up in England. Although she liked Australia she could never forget those wonderful Christmases of her childhood. It was at Christmas that she felt most lonely and often wished she was back in England.

'Ah well,' she sighed. 'At least it will soon be dark.'

Sure enough, the sky darkened and soon, although it was still warm, the sunlight faded and gave way to night.

'Christmas Eve,' thought Myra. 'I'd better get things ready.'

She went to her radio and turned it on. Soon the sound of carols filled the air. Next, Myra went to the cupboard under the stairs and got out a long cardboard box. Opening it she took out the beautiful candle that she only lit once a year. Putting it on the table in front of the window she lit it carefully and then sat back to listen to the carols by candlelight.

Now it so happened that on that Christmas Eve an Australian called Norman was walking along Myra's street. As he got near her house he heard the lovely sound of carols, and then he saw Myra sitting by the window in the flickering light of her beautiful candle.

Norman stood there for a few minutes.

'How lonely she looks,' he thought to himself. 'There are lots of people who live in Australia now but who were brought up in other countries. Perhaps more of them are lonely at Christmas.'

Then Norman had a brilliant idea. He had an interesting job working for a radio station and he knew lots of people would listen to his idea.

'How about this?' he said to them. 'I know there are lots of lonely people in our city of Melbourne at Christmas. You can see them listening to carols all by themselves. Why don't we organise a really terrific carol concert every Christmas Eve – and then anybody who wants to, can come and sing together.'

'Great idea,' said one of the important men, when he heard Norman's idea. And so started one of the world's biggest carol concerts. Every Christmas Eve in a huge theatre in Melbourne thousands of people gather to sing Christmas carols. For those who can't come the event is shown on television. Norman's great idea now gives pleasure to thousands of people, but he has never forgotten Myra. That's why the great concert is always called 'Carols by Candlelight.'

Prayer
Let us think this morning about how Christmas is celebrated by people all over the world. Let us think about the very first Christmas, when Jesus was born.

Hymn
'Go tell it on the mountain' (*Come and Praise* No 24)

Information for the teacher
1   This story is based on the experience of Norman Banks, a radio announcer who saw a lonely woman listening to carols by the light of a candle on Christmas Eve, 1937. He arranged the first community carol singing which has now grown into the Carols by Candlelight celebrations which are held every Christmas Eve in the Sydney Myer Music Bowl, Melbourne.

2   For more about Christmas in Australia and other countries, see 'Different Christmases' in *Christmas is Coming* by Redvers Brandling (Blackwell, 1985). An interesting talking point might be that people celebrate in many different ways – but they are all celebrating the *same* event.

Spring   *Special Occasions*

Introduction
Do you live near a park or a common? Or perhaps you live in the country? Today we are not going to have a story. Instead we are going to hear what a lady wrote in a book about one of the best times of the year – Spring.
   She tells us what Spring is like in a place near where she lives.

When you are listening to this, close your eyes and try to imagine all those birds and kites and people she talks about.

Spring

'It was getting on for Spring now and the Common was really coming to life. The prams with all the mothers were out in full force, being pushed about or parked beneath the trees round the bandstand.

The old men had brought along their chess or dominoes and were playing serious games while up above the chestnut leaves shook free from their sheaths, which fell upon the chequered boards. Soon the white and pink flowers would be in bloom.

The pigeons made a tremendous cooing, sparrows divebombed onto crumbs thrown by the mothers and the old duck built her nest as usual on the island of the small pond. All over the big pond, white sails sped by, or radio controlled steamers swept round in wide circles.

Cricket was replacing football in the fields, but fat schoolgirls in shorts were still leaping about netball courts. Children ran along, tugging at their kites which floated high on the winds. There was tremendous activity too across in the playground where children were swinging, riding, sliding and digging. In the little wood by the hard tennis courts, the grass was springing anew, a wonderful brilliant emerald, the bird cherries were out and the May bushes were in bud. The children ran out through the wood to see whether the caravans of the May fair had arrived yet, or wandered along to watch the workmen bulldozing the ground where the prefabs had stood. In every corner of the Common something was happening.

Elizabeth Stucley

Prayer

Let us give thanks for the beauty of our parks, commons, gardens and countryside when it is spring. Let us look carefully at blossom, early flowers, and trees, and enjoy their beauty.

Hymn

'Who put the colours in the rainbow' (*Come and Praise* No 12)

Information for the teacher

1   The great Hindu Spring Festival of Holi is one at which children have a lot of fun. It commemorates the time when Lord Krishna celebrated the first full moon of spring by throwing coloured powder over his friends. Coloured powder throwing is a highlight in modern celebrations as are bonfires, dancing and the eating of special food.

2   It could be pointed out to the children that spring is not only a very pleasant time of year but also a very important one for farmers. Various traditional rhymes stress the importance of March in particular:

'A dry March and a wet May
Fills barns and bags with corn and hay.

March damp and warm
Does farmers much harm.'

St Swithin   *Special Occasions*

Introduction
Swithin was a good, kind, helpful man who lived a very long time ago. He did so many kind things that all sorts of stories grew up about him.

This morning we are going to hear one of those stories. It begins with a poor old lady taking a basket of eggs to market.

Story
'What a crowd,' thought Martha as she walked to the market.

'That's good though,' she thought. 'With as many people as this about surely somebody will want to buy my eggs. Then I'll have enough money to buy food for my children.'

Martha was very poor. Her husband was dead and she had four hungry children to feed. The only way she could do this was by keeping a few hens and selling their eggs.

The road to the market got even more crowded and soon the walkers all came to a narrow bridge.

'I was here first,' said a big farmer, pushing another big farmer out of the way.

'No you were not,' replied the second man, and pushed back. Soon there was a crowd on the bridge. They all tried to push past the two farmers who were still arguing in the middle.

'I must get by,' thought Martha. 'I can't afford to be late for the market.' Squeezing by the side of the bridge she put her basket in front of her and edged forward. Then, suddenly, one of the farmers hit the other. He staggered back – and crashed into Martha's basket.

'Oh no!' she cried, but it was too late. The basket was knocked out of her hands. It fell sideways onto the bridge with a clatter, and all the eggs fell out and broke.

'My eggs, my eggs,' gasped Martha, and tears began to run down her cheeks. Now she had nothing to sell.

'My eggs,' she cried once again, and then sat on the bridge holding her face in her hands.

Seeing what had happened and feeling ashamed of themselves, the two farmers hurried off. Soon there was nobody on the bridge but Martha. She was still crying. Then she felt a hand on her shoulder.

'Don't cry,' a kind voice said. 'You stand up and we'll see what we can do.'

Martha looked up and there she saw a man everybody knew. His name was Swithin and he was known as the kindest man in the whole district.

'Now look,' went on Swithin. 'You hold the basket and I'll pass the eggs up to you.'

'But . . . ' began Martha, looking at the mess of smashed eggs.

'No 'buts', just get your basket ready,' said Swithin.

Then he picked up the first broken egg and handed it to Martha. An amazing thing happened. As the egg passed from Swithin's hand to Martha's – it suddenly became whole again. The same thing happened with every egg and soon Martha had a full basket again.

'I . . . I . . . just don't know how to thank you,' began Martha.

'I'm glad to have been able to help,' smiled Swithin, and he went on his way.

Prayer
A 'prayer' appropriate to this story is the short but succinct Islamic proverb: 'He is best loved who does most good to other creatures.'

Hymn
'A man for all the people' (*Come and Praise* No 27)

Information for the teacher
1   'St Swithin's Day if thou dost rain,
    For forty days it will remain,
    St Swithin's Day, if it be fair,
    For forty days 'twill rain no more.'

St Swithin's Day is 15 July and the story behind the old jingle is as follows. After a life of great attainments Swithin, then Bishop of Winchester, died in 862. He asked to be buried in a humble grave. In 1077 it was decided that such a great saint should have a splendid grave so work on reburial began. Immediately heavy rain began to fall – and persisted until the reburial attempts were abandoned. The rain was interpreted as a sign that Swithin did not want to be moved.

2   The story of Noah's Ark (Genesis 6–8) would fit in well with this assembly.

3   In Biblical times in Palestine water was very highly valued because it was so scarce. Sources of water determined where early settlements grew up, eg Jerusalem, Jericho. Water is mentioned in the Bible more than any other natural resource. It was not always freely available and in some cases was bought and sold. Water was essential in baptism to 'wash away' sin.

4   For some visual work to go with this information it might be useful to have a few examples from the Beaufort Notation:
d = drizzle;   h = hail;   L = lightning;   p = squalls;   r = rain;
rr = continuous rain; R = heavy rain; t = thunder.

Section 2
Class Assemblies

Introduction

In planning class assemblies it is vital to make sure that the presentations are visible and audible. I have found the arrangement below is effective when young children are involved in the presentations:

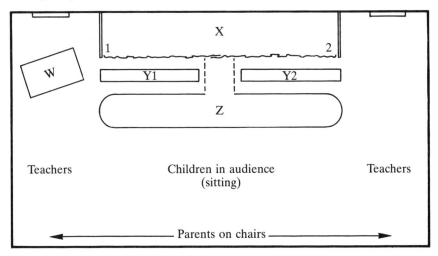

W – an area to one side of the presenting area where piano/musicians/choir etc can be located.

X – a curtained recess from behind which actors, props, speakers etc can be brought, or appear, when necessary.
(Should such a recess not be available, one can easily be created by putting some screens across the hall at points 1–2.)

Y1/Y2 – two sections with a passage between them for readers, announcers, speakers relating commentaries etc.

Z – the presenting area where the action takes place.

To further enhance good visibility and especially to encourage audibility, the selective use of staging blocks is recommended. This could mean individual blocks for speakers/readers or the arrangements of different levels when acting is taking place.

Encouraging young children to 'speak up' is more reliable than attempts at amplification 'on the day'. In direct contrast to this, of course, is the assembly which is pre-recorded, complete with speech, music and sound effects. This is then played at a suitably amplified level on the morning of the presentation and the action is all mimed to it.

1 A loaf of bread

Aim: to encourage an appreciation of growth, beginnings and how people help us.

Materials required: tray, stool, loaf of bread, cloth, lively introductory music.

Numbers involved: all the children in the class can participate in various ways.

Young children are very aware of the 'order of things'. This class assembly incorporates a variety of themes ranging from starting/growth to people who help us.

Presentation

The assembly begins with some bright and cheerful introductory music, to which the presenters make their entrance. One of them carries a tray – on which is a hidden object, covered by a cloth. Once everybody is in place the tray is put on a stool in a central position, and the cloth removed to reveal a loaf of bread. While attention is focused on this the following readings, (or statements) are made by various presenters:

Reader 1 We have brought a loaf of bread to show you.
Reader 2 Where does a loaf of bread start its life?
Reader 3 Where do we get it from?
Reader 4 Why do we need it?

After this, the following reading sets the scene for some dramatic action.

Reading This morning we are going to hear a poem. In a way this poem tells the story of a loaf of bread. It also tells us about people. You will need to listen and watch carefully. As each verse is read, watch the children acting out what it says.

At this point the presenting group re-arranges itself. (This will, of course, have been rehearsed in the pre-assembly preparation.) The five verses of the poem each have a separate reader; at the other side of the presenting area. While each verse is being read out, two or three of the other children act out the action of the verse. The teacher decides how the activity is to be done and which children take part – everybody can be involved.

The verses of the poem are as follows:

Sowing seed is my trade,
I grow corn and I get paid,
What I do helps us all,
Helps the truckman best of all.

Driving trucks is my trade,
I take sacks and I get paid,
What I do helps us all,
Helps the miller best of all.

Milling corn is my trade,
I make flour and I get paid,
What I do helps us all,
Helps the baker best of all,

Baking bread is my trade,
I make loaves and I get paid,
What I do helps us all,
Helps the shop man best of all.

Selling food is my trade,
All buy bread and I get paid,
Everyone needs food to live,
Everyone has help to give.

Anthony Geering

When the reading and action are completed, the assembly is concluded with a hymn and a prayer. A suitable hymn is: 'A Living Song' (*Come and Praise* No 72)
The concluding prayer might be:

This morning we have thought about the jobs people do to help us have food. Let us think about how important this is. Let us be thankful for those people and for what we eat. Let us end our service with two lines from the poem to remind us of these things:
'Everyone needs food to live,
Everyone has help to give.'

2 Let's be grateful

Aim: to make us realise that we often complain when we shouldn't, and that we should be more grateful for the good things in our lives.

Materials required: pieces of staging; pair of cymbals; pair of shoes.

Numbers involved: all the children in the class can participate; one particularly good reader is required.

Presentation

The assembly begins with the presenters moving, in twos and threes, into the presenting area. As they do so, members of each small group talk among themselves – loud enough for the rest of the people in the hall to hear. The basis of each little conversation is a 'grumble'. Examples might be:

Conversation 1
A Do you like school dinners?
B They're all right, but I wish we got more chips.
C We never get ice cream either do we?
B No we don't. I think they could be better.

Conversation 2
A My mum doesn't let me watch any more telly after we've had our tea.
B When do you have your tea?
A When my dad gets in.
B I can watch for ages after my tea.
A It's not fair.

Conversation 3
A I wish Miss would let me sit next to you in class.
B So do I. I don't know why she doesn't.
A She says we talk too much if we sit together.
B I think it's rotten. We should be allowed to sit together.
A Yes we should.

Obviously these little preambles will have been carefully rehearsed, as will the movements which eventually get all the conversationalists into their pre-arranged places in the presenting area. Once this has been done, a pair of cymbals clashes off-stage, to focus attention on a significant change in the assembly's mood.

Immediately after the noise of the cymbals one of the children enters and moves to centre stage, very obviously carrying a pair of shoes. These are then laid prominently on a piece of staging and the following readings take place:

Reading 1 This morning we have heards lots of grumbling.
Reading 2 We all grumble at times.
Reading 3 Perhaps we grumble too much. We should be more grateful for the good things in our lives.
Reading 4 This pair of shoes (*Points at shoes*) reminds us of a man who was always grumbling . . .
Reading 5 Until . . .

At this point a narrator takes his or her place on another piece of staging and reads the following story. While this is being read other children mime the action to the appropriate words. Little rehearsal will have been needed here because both story and action are uncomplicated.

Story:

There was once a man who was always grumbling. He lived in a hot country where people wore long, loose clothes. One day he looked at his shoes and thought: 'They are nearly worn out and I have no money to buy a new pair. It just isn't fair!'

That day he went to his church. As he knelt there praying he looked at the man next to him. His long clothes covered all his kneeling body.

'I bet he's got plenty of money,' thought the grumbler. 'I bet he can afford a new pair of shoes.'

When the church service ended two men came across and picked up the man next to the grumbler. As they did so the grumbler saw that the man was a cripple who had no feet. At once the grumbler felt terribly ashamed, and from that day on he never grumbled again.

The assembly could then end with everybody singing: 'Fill your hearts with joy and gladness' (*Come and Praise* No 9)

3 'This is your life'

Aim: to show the value of ordinary people.

Materials required: A big red file/book; a portable microphone; chairs for a group of people in a simulated *This is your life* presentation.

Numbers involved: whole class participation in prayers and hymns; smaller group involved in the rest of the action; there is a good opportunity to involve a parent here.

The idea behind this assembly is a *This is your life* presentation. It is best to have the teacher as the interviewer, with the subject of the profile being a child from the class. The people to be interviewed are initially strategically placed among the audience. One of those to be interviewed can be an adult if pre-assembly presentation can cater for this. The action, while obviously rehearsed, then appears to evolve quite naturally.

Presentation

The assembly begins with some fanfare-type introductory music. The teacher/interviewer, holding red book and microphone, enters centre stage.

Teacher: 'Ladies and gentlemen, This is your life! This morning we are going to interview . . . (*long pause*) . . . Joanne Green!'

At this stage the interviewer turns dramatically to one of the children gathered in the presenting group. This is 'Joanne Green', who gasps something like: 'But why me? I'm just ordinary.'

Interviewer: 'Ordinary? I don't think so. Let's go and see what Rachid Murani has to say about that.' (*Interviewer then moves into the audience and speaks to Rachid*).

Rachid: 'I only moved to this school two weeks ago. I was very scared. Everything seemed so different from my last school. The first person to speak to me was Joanne – and she gave me one of her sweets. That made me feel much better.'

Interviewer: 'Thank you Rachid. Would you go and sit on the platform please. Now let's find out what Julie Clarke has to say.' (*Interviewer moves to next pre-located child*)

Julie: 'I have known Joanne since we were at playschool. She is a really good friend. I can tell her all my troubles and she never laughs at me. She never says horrible things about people.'

Interviewer: 'Thank you Julie – would you go and sit on the platform please? Now let's talk to Derek. (*Moves to Derek*)

Interviewer: 'Derek – could I ask you a few questions please?'

Derek: 'Yes.'

Interviewer: 'Would you say that Joanne was very good at writing?'

Derek: 'No, not really.'

Interviewer: 'Is she one of the best writers in your class?'

Derek: 'No.'

Interviewer: 'Do you think Joanne finds it easy to write letters?'

Derek: 'No, very hard.'

Interviewer: 'Could you tell us more please?'

Derek: 'I had to go into hospital to have my tonsils out. When I was in hospital I got a letter from Joanne. She told me what was happening at school and in our street. There were a few mistakes in the letter and it must have taken her ages to write it. It was great to get it though.'

Interviewer: 'Thank you Derek, please take a seat on the platform. Now I wonder what Mrs Patel can tell us.' (*Moves to Mrs Patel*)

Mrs Patel: 'Joanne sometimes comes to play with my daughter Beejal. Beejal's grandmother lives with us and she doesn't speak very much English. Joanne brought her easy reading book round with her, showed my mother the pictures and read the words underneath them. My mother thinks she is such a nice, kind girl.'

Interviewer: 'Thank you Mrs Patel, would you please join us on the platform.' (*Interviewer and Mrs Patel join the others*)

Interviewer: 'Ladies and gentlemen, from what you have heard I am sure you will agree that 'ordinary' is not the best word to describe Joanne Green. This one is much better.'

At this point the interviewer holds out an indicative arm and four children among the presenters turn round large cards they have been holding. Each card contains a large letter and together they spell out: **kind**.

The interviewer then presents the red book to Joanne Green and says, 'Thank you Joanne, this is your life.' At this point one of the presenters steps forward and after saying 'Let us pray,' reads the following prayer:

'Let us be thankful for all those people around us who find time to say a kind word to us, who are never too busy to listen or help, who care about others.'

The assembly could then be concluded by everybody singing: 'Lord of all hopefulness' (*Come and Praise* No 52)

4 St Lucy

Aim: to remind us of brave people who help others.

Materials required: a real candle; a 'crown' of cardboard candles; a white dress; coffee; small cakes; kettle and paper cups.

Numbers involved: whole class participation; parent visitors can also be involved as recipients.

Preparation: part of the 'action' of this assembly involves preparing coffee. Obviously, this should only be simulated in the presentation, but real coffee can be substituted at an appropriate point, to be distributed to parents and teachers in the audience.

13 December commemorates St Lucy's Day and this occasion is marked with festivities in Sweden. Early December is therefore the ideal calendar location for this assembly, but such is its theme that it could be used equally well at any time during the school year.

Presentation

Any suitable introductory music could provide a background while the audience comes in. Once they have settled, most of the presenters take up their positions, but a small group remains out of sight – ready to appear at the appropriate moment. The teacher then begins the assembly with the following introduction:

Teacher: Good morning, everybody. Every year, in a country called Sweden, people remember a very brave little girl. This morning we are going to tell you how they do this – and why they do it. The girl's name was Lucy, and many people remember her by . . (*At this point the teacher lights a candle and places it in a holder at one side of the stage.*) This is what children do on the special day which is called St Lucy's Day.

The teacher steps out of the way and a reader takes over.
Reader: 'Girls get up and dress like this.'

There then enter two or three girls dressed completely in white.

Reader: 'Their brothers put special crowns of candles on their heads.'

Enter 'brothers' who put previously prepared cardboard crowns of candles on each of the girls' heads.

Reader: 'Their Dads make coffee.'

Enter 'dads' who simulate boiling kettle, spooning coffee into paper cups, adding milk etc, setting out the 'coffee' on trays.

Reader: 'Their Mums get out the cakes.'

Enter 'mums' with a tin of individual cakes which are also put on the trays.

Reader: 'Then the boys and girls go out and visit people.

The crowned girls in white dresses move off, followed by the boys bearing the trays of coffee and cakes. They move to where the parents/teachers are sitting and the girls hand the drinks and cakes round. When the action is finished the reader continues.

Reader: 'These girls have been reminding everybody of St Lucy. St Lucy lived a very long time ago and we remember her because she was very brave.'

At this point two more readers replace their earlier counterpart. The assembly progresses with these two telling the 'Lucy' story in tandem. As a useful adjunct to this, another child could hold up of one or two large pictures denating scenes from the story.

Reader 1: 'Lucy lived at a time when Christians were in great danger.'
Reader 2: 'Sometimes Christians had to hide from soldiers who wanted to capture them.'
Reader 1: 'Lucy knew about some Christians who were hiding.'
Reader 2: 'Every day she took food to their dark hiding place.
Reader 1: 'So that she could use two hands to carry food she wore a crown of candles to light her way.'
Reader 2: 'Lucy saved many people's lives in this way.'

When this point of the assembly has been reached everyone bows their heads for the reading of the following prayer:

'Let us think today about Lucy, a very brave girl. Let us also think about other brave people, all over the world, who risk their own lives to help others.

The assembly could end with the singing of 'The Family of Man' (*Come and Praise* No 69)

5 Working together

Aim: to emphasise the value of co-operation, combining talents and working together.

Materials required: two large cardboard silhouettes of ships; a number of name cards (as indicated in the text).

Numbers involved: whole class participation.

This assembly focuses on the well-known saying 'no man is an island'. It seeks to remind children that by combining their qualities and talents they are much more able to cope with difficult occasions when they arise.

Presentation

The assembly could begin with some stirring 'sea-faring' music – the overture from Wagner's *Flying Dutchman* is a good choice here, if available. The presenters take up their positions during this musical introduction, and sit in a very formal arrangement facing the audience. When the music stops a reader begins:

'Good morning, everybody. This morning we want to begin by telling you something about our class.'

There is then a long recital of appearances, qualities, preferences etc related to the children in the class. As each of these is stated the children concerned stand up – sitting down again immediately afterwards, so that those referred to next can take their places. All the children should be involved in standing up several times. Some of the items mentioned could be:

'There are people who have blue eyes and are in our class. (*Children with blue eyes stand*)
There are people who have brown eyes. (*Brown eyes stand, and so on*)
There are people with green or hazel eyes.
There are people who have one or more brothers.
There are people who have one or more sisters.
There are people who like drawing better than anything else.
There are people who like singing better than anything else.
There are people who are good at PE and Games . . .'

The list is continued according to the class teacher's choice. At its conclusion, one of the presenters says:

> 'Now you know a lot about us. We work together and we play together. We are friends and help each other and we could all sail in this ship.'

At this point in the proceedings two of the presenters reach behind the curtains and bring out the first ship silhouette, which has the name *HMS Friendship* written on it in large letters.

We know the crew of this ship very well. They are: (*Cards with names printed on them are then shown*) Captain Kind; Lieutenant Help; Mr Thoughtful; Mr Smiling; Mr Cheerful; Mr Reliable.

At this point in the assembly everybody joins in the singing of a hymn – perhaps 'The Family of Man' (*Come and Praise* No 69). Following the hymn one of the presenters continues:

> 'It is because we are good friends, know and help each other that we do not worry too much when we meet *this* ship.'

At this stage another ship silhouette is brought into view with the name *HMS Hardship* written on it. The crew's names are displayed in a similar manner to the first one. Captain Surly; Lieutenant Loneliness; Mr Mean; Mr Bully; Mr Selfish; Mr Greedy.

The assembly is then concluded by the presenters speaking in unison and saying the following prayer:

> Every day we work and play
> We help each other on our way.
> Friends we make at school and home
> Help us when outside we roam.

6 Sharing

Aim: to show how food helps us to share celebrations with each other.

Materials required: a birthday cake (or model of one). Other items of food, if prepared in advance (see below).

Numbers involved: the whole class is involved in the presentation. Depending on numbers, the rest of the school could be the audience.

Preparation: An essential piece of pre-assembly preparation is to find somebody who has a birthday on the day of the presentation. This could be a child in the school, a parent, grandparent or teacher – even one of the school pets, if human birthdays are not convenient!

For a more ambitious assembly, different kinds of 'celebratory' food could be prepared in advance. The teacher might ask one or two of the parents, or the school cook, to make charoset, hot cross buns, chapattis . . . (recipes are given at the end of these notes).

As adults, we know that eating together at a celebration reduces tension between very different kinds of people and offers meeting points which promote friendship and understanding. This is also a very worthwhile theme to pursue with young children – particularly in a multi-ethnic situation. The following assembly outline will obviously be adapted by teachers to suit their own ethnic mix or situation. Some teachers may seek to develop the theme in a much more ambitious way than others; the size of the school could be a significant factor here.

Presentation

An obvious choice of introductory music is a recording of 'Food, glorious food' from the musical *Oliver*. During the music, the presenting class take up their positions. Once they are ready, the first presenter says:

Presenter 1 Today is a special day for Ian. (*or whoever*) It is his birthday.
Presenter 2 Ian will have some special food at his party tonight.
Presenter 1 Ian will have a birthday cake.

At this point a real, or model, birthday cake is brought on to the presenting area, and candles are put on it.

Presenter 2 When it is somebody's birthday we share the cake.
Presenter 1 Everybody at a birthday party gets a piece of cake.

If the teacher feels it is practicable a sharing of the cake ceremony takes place. A pre-recorded message could then be played, saying something like:

When it is somebody's birthday we celebrate together by sharing the cake and other food. There are other times when we celebrate by eating together. Watch, we are going to show you some.

Pre-arranged groups then hold up cards with celebratory titles written on them. As each title appears, other members of the group move towards it, holding up drawings and names of appropriate food, eg:

Christmas: a Christmas pudding and mince pies
Easter: hot cross buns
Passover: charoset
Hanukkah: latkes
Diwali: chapattis

If any of this food has been prepared in advance it could now be introduced, and distributed in tiny pieces to children, parents and teachers present.

Once the food distribution is over the following passage could be read by a teacher or parent:

Food is heaven.
As you cannot go to heaven alone,
Food is to be shared.
Food is heaven.

(Part of a prayer by Kim Chi Ha, from *Declaration of Conscience*, Korea)

The assembly ends with everybody singing: 'Thank you Lord' (*Come and Praise* No 32)

This assembly offers an enormous number of follow-up possibilities back in the classroom. The need for sensitivity with regard to taboo foods for children of various religions should, of course, always be borne in mind.

Recipes:

Charoset:
chopped nuts; grated cooking apple; cinnamon; lemonade.
Mix ingredients and bind into a paté with the liquid.

Chapattis:
wholemeal flour and warm water are mixed, kneaded, left. They are then kneaded again, rolled into small balls, flattened and rolled again. They are then put on a griddle for a few seconds and when a 'puffed' effect is achieved they are served.

Hot Cross Buns:

300g (¾ lb) flour; 12g (½oz) yeast; 25g (1 oz) sugar; 125 ml (¼pt) tepid milk/water mix; 1 egg; 35g (1½oz) currants; 25g (1oz) candied peel; ¼ teaspoonful grated nutmeg; ¼ teaspoonful ground cinnamon; 25g (1oz) margarine; pinch of salt; milk and sugar to glaze.

1 Sieve ¾ lb of flour into a basin. Cream the yeast with a teaspoon of sugar, add tepid liquid. Strain into sieved flour and mix.
2 Cover with cloth, put in warm place for 20 minutes.
3 During this time sieve the remaining flour with salt, sugar and add currants, chopped peel, nutmeg and cinnamon. Melt the margarine and beat the egg.
4 When first mixture has risen stir in dry ingredients, pour in melted margarine and beaten egg. Mix, knead thoroughly.
5 Cover with cloth, put in warm place for an hour.
6 Shape portions of dough into round buns. Put these on a well-greased and floured baking tin, allowing them to spread.
7 Cut a cross on top of each bun and then put back in warm place for 15 minutes.
8 Bake in hot oven: 450°F (230°C) Gas Mark 8, for 20 minutes.
9 When buns are brown, glaze with milk and sugar.
10 Allow to cool.

7 The spacemen's Christmas

Aim: to give a little originality to a Christmas assembly for infants.

Materials required: Space and Nativity costumes; basic sets for mimes (if required, but these are not essential). Tape recorder and pre-recorded tape.

Numbers involved: whole class participation.

This assembly is in two parts; the second part can be extended as the teacher wishes.

Presentation

The assembly could start with some traditional carols being played. This is likely to lead the audience to assume that some rather predictable Christmas presentation is about to take place. When the audience is seated, however, the carols are suddenly replaced by a pre-recorded tape with 'sound effects' of a spaceship going out of control: the panic-stricken crew shouting instructions to each other; the final crash.

After the crash there is a moment of silence on the tape, followed by some conversation:

> We've landed.
> Is anyone hurt?
> I don't think so.
> I wonder where we are?
> Let's get out and see.

At this point the curtains or screens part and four or five suitably-dressed space people appear. As they do so, the carols are heard again. The space travellers begin to speak:

Zak We're on a place called Earth.
Pik It said on the computer before we landed that it was Christmas on Earth.
Luk I wonder what happens then?
Lem Why don't we watch while Zin is mending our spaceship?
Zak Somebody's coming – let's make ourselves disappear.

The space travellers press a button to make themselves disappear – but in reality just move to the side of the stage.

Next several groups of presenters mime or act out some modern Christmas scenes. These could include: decorating a Christmas tree; carol singing; a Christmas party; hanging up stockings; opening presents; visiting Santa Claus.

When this activity is over the space travellers 'beam themselves back' to centre stage and resume their conversation.

Zak The humans seem to enjoy this Christmas.

Pik It's a very special time.

Luk It said on the computer that it is something to do with a baby being born.

(*Voice of Zin offstage*) Spaceship repaired and ready to go, Captain.

Lem Good – why don't we travel back to that place called Bethlehem and see what happened?

Zak Good idea – let's go.

The space travellers disappear behind curtains or screens and some taped take-off sounds are heard.

The travellers then re-appear.

Zak Here we are in Bethlehem for the first Christmas. Let's see what happens.

The following poem is read by a teacher or parent (or played on a tape-recorder). Groups of children present simple, mimed re-enactment of the events of the Nativity, which relate to each of the verses:

> Mary set out on a winter's night,
> Joseph by her side to give her light,
> They'd many long miles to go that night,
> Before they reached the town O,
> Town O town O,
> They'd many long miiles to go that night,
> Before they reached the town O.
>
> They walked 'til they came to the first big inn,
> Knocked at the door, 'Will you let us in?
> We've come many miles to Bethlehem,
> In order to be counted,
> Counted, counted,
> We've come many miles to Bethelehem,
> In order to be counted.'
>
> The innkeeper looked at them both and said,
> 'I've no room,' and he shook his head,
> 'There's many come to sleep and be fed,
> And all my rooms are taken,
> Taken, taken,

There's many come to sleep and be fed,
And all my rooms are taken.'

They tried everywhere but they all said 'No,'
It seemed to them both they had no place to go,
'Til at last a man smiled and said, 'I know,
Come spend the night in my stable,
Stable, stable,
'Til at last a man smiled and said, 'I know,
Come spend the night in my stable.'

The shelter was cold and the stable bare,
Yet here was a man who seemed to care,
And on that night to that lonely pair,
A baby was born called Jesus,
Jesus, Jesus,
And on that night to that lonely pair,
A baby was born called Jesus.

Susan Moxom

When this is finished the various presenters mass on the presenting area and everybody joins in the singing of an appropriate Christmas carol.

8   Diwali

Aim: there are several aims to this assembly:
- **to reinforce our appreciation of 'home'**
- **to consider celebration when we return home after an absence**
- **to introduce Diwali**

Materials required: painted (or crayoned) cut-out lamps for all the presenters.

Numbers involved: whole class participation

Presentation

The assembly begins with the audience taking their places without any background music. Similarly the presenters move into place silently. The presenters then begin the following chant:

Presenters: Hari Krishna, Hari Krishna,
Krishna, Krishna, Hari, Hari.

Hari Rama, Hari Rama,
Rama, Rama, Hari, Hari.
(Obviously this will have been rehearsed beforehand; it can be accompanied by hand-clapping and very simple percussion. In keeping with tradition, as the chant is repeated it increases in speed.)

This unusual start to the assembly is brought to a sudden stop after the tempo has been built up over three or four choruses. Presenters then read, or say, the following:

Presenters: After school we go home
We like going home.
On special occasions we have parties at home.
At this stage another round of *Hari Krishna* could be chanted.

Presenters: This morning we are going to tell you a story.
The story is about a prince called Rama.
He had been away from home for a very long time.
After many adventures all his people wanted him to come home.
They went to meet him.
They took thousands of lamps to light his way home.
These lamps were called *diva*.

At this stage a very simple mimed dramatisation takes place. Rama and Sita are seen in the woods, then the rest of the presenters form a path, holding out their model *diva* to light the way home for the prince and his wife. As this action is taking place another round of *Hari Krishna* is chanted.

After this little dramatic scene the commentary continues:

Presenters: We often have a party when somebody comes home after being away for a very long time.
There was a party for Prince Rama and Princess Sita.
There were presents.
There was special food.
There were cards.
There were coloured lights.
Every year many people remember the party for Rama and Sita and they have a party too.

Another little mime takes place at this stage with presents and Diwali cards being exchanged. Some Indian music on record would add to the atmosphere here and the diva could be much in evidence again. Whilst the action is taking place, six of the presenters could hold up six large letters which spell out *Diwali*.

To conclude this scene and to provide a complete contrast the teacher then asks everybody to bow their heads for a prayer:

This morning we have been thinking about a special festival called Diwali. Festivals are times when people remember very special happenings. Let us give thanks for those times when we enjoy ourselves.

The presenters might then conclude the assembly by asking the audience to join them in one or two more Hari Krishna choruses. One of the offshoots of this assembly is that it provides plenty of opportunity for classroom follow-up work on the story of Rama, Sita and Ravana.

9   Guru Nanak and the carpet

Aim: using a religious story to show how a present could be best used.

Materials required: a rug, a model (or toy) dog.

Numbers involved: whole class participation

Presentation

This assembly is based on a Sikh story about Guru Nanak. It could begin with the presenters singing 'Happy Birthday' as the audience take their places in the hall. Once they are in position the assembly progresses as follows:

Speaker 1:   When it is somebody's birthday we give them a present.
Speaker 2:   This morning's story is about a very wise old man.
Speaker 1:   His name was Guru Nanak.
Speaker 2:   Guru Nanak was always trying to help people.
Speaker 1:   He used these to help poor people.
Speaker 1:   So people sent him money and other presents all the time.
Speaker 2:   Then a man called Nuri heard of Guru Nanak.
Nuri: Good morning everybody. I am called Nuri and I am a carpet weaver. I have made a magnificent carpet.

At this point in the assembly Nuri goes behind the curtains or screen and, with some helpers, brings out a carpet. As it appears, the presenters all move into small groups and mutter to each other:

Everyone 'Isn't it marvellous . . . what a lovely carpet . . . what are you going to do with it, Nuri?'

Nuri then speaks to everybody and says:

Nuri: I have heard that Guru Nanak is a great and kind man. I am going to give him this carpet as a present. It is the best one I have ever made. Can somebody tell me where I can find him?

One of the presenters takes Nuri by the hand and, with the carpet bearers following, leads him in and out of the presenters until they part and reveal Guru Nanak sitting cross-legged on the ground. The dialogue then continues:

Nuri: Master, I have heard of all the kind things you do. Would you allow me to give you this carpet so that you will always be comfortable as you sit on it.

Guru Nanak: What a lovely carpet.
Guru Nanak: I thank you Nuri . . . but I cannot sit on the carpet . . .
Nuri: But . . .
Guru Nanak: Over there you see a small dog. *(Guru points and
                presenters move aside to reveal the toy or model dog,
                which has been placed in position previously.)*
                That dog is cold and starving. He will die unless he
                has something warm to cover him. Please put your
                carpet over him.
Nuri: Yes Master.

The teacher then says a prayer appropriate to this assembly:

Let us think this morning about giving and getting presents. Let
us pray that presents are used well to give pleasure and help.
Let us always try to be kind in thoughts, words and deeds.

The assembly is concluded by everybody singing: 'Lord of all hopefulness'
(*Come and Praise* No 52)

The possibilities for classroom follow-up work related to this assembly
include the telling of more Guru Nanak stories. A good source of these is
Robert Fisher's excellent assembly book: *The Assembly Year* (Collins
Educational 1985).

10   The Bully

Aim: to encourage children to care for each other; to disparage bullying.

Materials required: a 'dummy' child (paper-stuffed clothes, painted mask face etc) sitting in a central position in the presenting area; some large individual cards bearing letters which make up the word **BULLY**.

Numbers involved: whole class, divided into pre-arranged groups.

Presentation

Ideally this assembly could start with the BBC record of children singing hymns from *Come and Praise* as the audience take their places in the hall. While this is happening the presenters bring in the dummy figure, seat him in a central and prominent position and then arrange themselves in groups. The teacher begins the assembly by saying:

> Good morning, everybody. This morning we just couldn't get anybody to play the part of the main character in our assembly. Nobody would do it! You'll see why when we tell you his name.

The first group of presenters then make their way to the front of the presenting area. The biggest boy among them pushes the other children around and generally makes himself objectionable. After this little mimed drama, one of the presenters holds up a large card with **B** on it, and another says:

> He is big and he always pushes us about.

All the children in this group then point their fingers at the dummy and say in unison:

> The first letter of his name is **B**.

The first group retires and group two move to the foreground. Again a little mimed drama takes place: some boys and girls are playing in a playground, but one of them is continually going round doing spiteful things – pulling hair, tripping people up, giving sly kicks etc. When this mime ends, one of this group holds up a card showing the letter U, and another says:

> He is always going around doing unpleasant things.

This group then all point their fingers at the dummy and say:

> The second letter of his name is **U**.

Once the second group have completed their scene, the third group go straight into a mime which shows an injured child on the ground. Several of the others are helping, but one is standing to one side pointing and laughing at the victim's misfortune. A third card bearing the letter **L** is held up, with the accompanying comment:

> He is the sort of person who laughs when someone else has been hurt.

The group point at the dummy and say:

> The third letter of his name is **L**.

The fourth group's mime shows a group of children arguing over a book or comic. Two of them pull and tug at this until it tears. Then a teacher appears on the scene. One of the two antagonists immediately shakes their head and points at the other to indicate blame. Again a card showing the letter **L** is held up with the two comments:

He tells lies to get other people into trouble.

> The fourth letter of his name is **L**.

When the fifth group of presenters make their way to the forefront, the audience will obviously be expecting more of the same – so it would be a good idea to surprise them. This time, the presenters all point out into the audience and say:

> Perhaps you have done some of the nasty things we have been telling about, or you have . . . or you have.

After a few indiscriminate indications like this the final card appears with the letter **Y** and the comment:

> The last letter of his name is **Y**.

The teacher finishes with a prayer:

> None of us wanted to play the part of Bully because none of us wanted to be called that. At times, however, we all do unkind things, so let us pray this morning that we find much more time to care about each other rather than to hurt each other in any way. Let us pray too that all bullies realise how miserable they make other people, and that they try to be kinder and more thoughtful.

The assembly ends with everybody singing 'The family of man' (*Come and Praise* No 69).

Section 3
Drama in Assembly

Introduction

(Drama) provides an outlet for self expression and helps the development of imagination and artistic awareness; it increases social awareness (particularly through role play), mental awareness, fluency of speech, self knowledge, self respect, self discipline and self confidence. It gives children the opportunity to learn how to co-operate with others and helps develop orderly thinking and the ability to organise . . . It may also have a therapeutic effect, through helping children to deal with real life problems, or a carthartic effect, by enabling them to act out violence and frustration. It provides social and moral training.

(*100+ Ideas for Drama*, Anna Scher and Charles Verrall)

Clearly, there is much to commend the use of drama in infant and first school assemblies. In class assemblies, drama is the rule rather than the exception; it is often possible for a single presenter to spontaneously involve children to illuminate a story.

As previously stated, drama can be used in an action/reading context; in a series of mimes supported by commentaries; or in a more detailed manner, whereby casting, scripting and rehearsing have all been done in detail before the presentation. Obviously, preparation time for these three types of presentation will vary enormously and will depend, to a great extent, on the individual teacher's choice.

To correspond with these three uses of drama, the suggestions in this chapter are divided into three sections:

1 Ideas for drama, which can be developed as and how the teacher chooses.
2 Suggestions about how two of these items could be developed, with pointers indicating how they might be used in easily-prepared acting/miming situations, supported by read commentaries.

3   Guidelines on how a further two items might be extended into a prepared
    play: writing a script; casting; learning words; rehearsal. The end product
    here will be a prepared play – the highlight of the assembly presentation
    in which it is featured.

1 Ideas for drama

This is simply a list of ideas which have dramatic potential for assembly. The list covers not only simple starters but possibilities linked to special occasions and the Bible.

Simple starters

Getting a letter
The new baby
The new pet
When Mum was ill
Brothers and sisters
Gran and Grandad
Having a tea party
Sharing
The bully
'Teasing isn't nice'
'I thought you were my friend'
'Thank you for helping me'
The big surprise
Telling lies
Saying unkind things
Telling tales
Gossip
The lost pet
People who help us
Accidents will happen
'Don't cry'

'Help!'
'I didn't think I could do it until I tried.'
'It's all your own fault.'
The good idea
'Something has been stolen'
'Isn't he/she a nice person.'
Two's company
Its the thought that counts
Merry Christmas
All that glitters is not gold
Actions speak louder than words
'I don't believe it.'
'At last!'
The knock at the door
My happiest moment
The funniest (saddest, most important, most unusual etc.)
thing that has ever happened in our house
Caring for pets
Doing a good turn
If I had to give somebody a present (Mum, Dad, somebody
who is ill, a Third World refugee, Jesus–if he was here today,
a handicapped person.)
Things that annoy me
Being brave (at the dentist's, if the house catches fire, if
somebody is hurt, when Mum is in hospital etc)
Lovely things (seasons, town, country etc)
What I want to be when I grow up
My favourite food
What I like doing best
Something made me very sad
Lending and borrowing (without asking; broken on return?)
Making friends
Having an argument
In the classroom
When the spaceship came

Dramatic possibilities linked to special occasions

Throughout the year there are many religious and secular occasions and
anniversaries which have dramatic potential. The following month-by-month
list includes some of these, but the teacher will probably want to add more.

(The Commission for Racial Equality publishes a very useful annual publication called *The Calendar of Religious Festivals*; contact CRE, Elliot House, 10–12 Allington Street, London SW1E 5EH)

September

Religious occasions:

Harvest festival	gathering in the harvest; machines in action; different kinds of harvest – fish, coal etc
Rosh Hashanah (Jewish New Year)	joyful celebration welcomed by blowing a ram's horn (*shofar*). On New Year's Eve people eat apples dipped in honey – symbol of a 'sweet' new year
Sukkot (Jewish Feast of Tabernacles)	celebrated with offerings of grapes, fruits, olives and palms. Children are given sweets, fruit and flags; festivities involve dancing
Dusshera	a Hindu celebration of events in the life of Rama (see class assembly on Rama and Sita, page 154). Mainly Northern India

Secular occasions:
- Battle of Marathon 490 BC. News of the Greek victory over the Persians was carried by a Greek soldier to Athens – a run of 25 miles (40km); the first 'marathon'
- Outbreak of plague at Eyam in Derbyshire, 1665
- The Great Fire of London, 2 Sept 1666
- First run of Stephenson's *Rocket* on the Manchester-Liverpool railway, 1830
- Grace Darling's lifeboat rescue, 1838

October

Religious occasions:

Feast of St Francis of Assisi	Saint Francis is the patron saint of creatures. Festival is celebrated on 4 October
Diwali (Hindu Festival of Lights)	celebrated in October or November. Theme of making things brighter – related to Rama and Sita story. Features lights (lamps and candles); new clothes; presents; music; fireworks; open-air dancing

| *Halloween* | actually the eve of All Saints' Day, but usually celebrated in secular fashion, with 'trick or treat', bobbing for apples, ghost stories, turnip lanterns . . . |

Secular occasions:
- *11 Oct* (1982) Raising of the *Mary Rose* – Tudor ship which sank on 19 Sept 1545
- *24 Oct* United Nations Day
- *29 Oct* (1910) Jean Henri Dunant, founder of Red Cross organisation, died
- Jonathan Swift, author of *Gulliver's Travels*, died 1745
- Lord Shaftesbury, social reformer, died in 1885 – possibilities here for a 'This is your life' presentation featuring an exploited child of the nineteenth century compared with a modern child

November

Religious occasions:

| *Advent Sunday* | the nearest Sunday to 30 Nov; marks the start of preparations for Christmas. Possible dramatic links with 'Beginnings' |
| *Hanukkah* (Jewish Festival of Lights) | celebrated by lighting candles in the nine-branched *menorah*; playing with a *dreidle* (a kind of spinning top); eating potato pancakes (*latkes*) |

Secular occasions:
- *5 Nov* Guy Fawkes Night (Bonfire night); celebration of the unsuccessful Gunpowder Plot in 1605
- *5 Nov* (1872) the *Marie Celeste* set sail from New York and was later found deserted
- *12 Nov* (1035) King Canute died – good 'moral' dramatic possibilities connected with the story of the waves (see page 180)
- *18 Nov* (1307) traditionally the day on which William Tell shot the apple from his son's head
- Lord Mayor's Show, London (second Saturday)
- Remembrance Sunday (nearest Sunday to 11 Nov) – celebration of the Armistice of 1918; parades, church services; 'poppies'
- SOS became the internationally-accepted distress signal Nov 1906. ('Mayday' comes from the French m'aidez or help me)

December

Religious occasions:

Christingle services   of Moravian Church origin, the services initially took place on Christmas Eve. Every child given a 'Christingle' – an orange (the world) with a candle in the top (the light of the world). Four cocktail sticks with nuts and raisins on them are attached (the four seasons) and a red ribbon tied around the orange (blood Jesus shed for the world)

Feast of St Nicholas   patron saint of children; the original Santa Claus (see also page 174)

St Lucia's Day   13 December. St Lucia hid Christians who were being persecuted. To free her hands to carry food to them, she wore a head-dress of candles to light her way.

Secular occasions:

- *17 Dec* (1903) Wright brothers' first successful aeroplane flight, Kittyhawk, USA
- *20 Dec* (1981) Penlee lifeboat disaster – 8 lifeboatmen died in an attempt to rescue seamen from the *Union Star*. 8 sailors also died
- *24 Dec* (1918) 'Silent Night' was first sung (see page 123)
- *28 Dec* (1879) Tay Bridge disaster – the inadequately-built bridge collapsed as a train crossed, killing all passengers (good dramatic link with 'foundations')
- *Nov 1660* First actress appeared on the British stage (previously boys had played women's parts)
- *Nov 1795* birth of Sir Roland Hill, founder of the Post Office

January

Religious occasions:

Epiphany   celebrated on 6 Jan – the twelfth night after Christmas. Christian celebration of Jesus' presentation to the Magi and symbolic gifts –gold for a king; frankincense for a priest; myrrh for suffering.

Secular occasions:
- *4 Jan* (1785) Jacob Grimm, co-author of *Grimm's Fairy Tales* born
- *10 Jan* (1840) Sir Rowland Hill founded Penny Post
- *10 Jan* (1917) Buffalo Bill (William Frederick Cody) died. His job was to feed railroad workers building the lines across America. In doing so he killed 5000 buffalo in 18 months
- *29 Jan* (1856) Victoria Cross established (a useful link with *The soldier who would not fight* page 16)
- January 1908, Baden Powell founded the Boy Scouts

February/March

Religious occasions:

Candlemas	celebrated on 2 Feb. Commemorates presentation of Jesus at the temple. Candles blessed in churches and distributed to members of the congregation
Shiva Ratri (Hindu festival of the Dance of Shiva)	Shiva, one of the three most important Hindu gods, is celebrated in dance and drama. Shiva traditionally dances on the back of ignorance, which must be destroyed so that people can be enlightened. Useful link with celebration through dance
St Valentine's Day	14 Feb. Secular associations with love and Valentine cards. There were two St Valentines – both killed for being Christians. The most famous famous one was an Italian priest, imprisoned for sheltering Christians who restored the sight of a warden's daughter
Shrove Tuesday	commonly 'Pancake Day' – the time for using up fat and eggs before fasting during the 40 days of Lent
Ash Wednesday	ashes made from the burnt palm crosses of the previous year are sprinkled with water and blessed, then daubed on the forehead as a sign of repentance
Mothering Sunday	the fourth Sunday in Lent – children give flowers, cards and presents to their mothers

Purim	Jewish commemoration of Esther's triumph over Haman. Processions, music, plays. Children are encouraged to make rude noises when the name of Haman is mentioned in services. Special food is eaten – *hamantashen* (pastries containing poppy seeds)
Holi (Hindu Spring Festival)	a time of high spirits and good humour, expressed by throwing coloured powder over other people, as Lord Krishna did
Palm Sunday	commemorates Jesus' entry into Jerusalem. People are given palm crosses in church services. (Strong dramatic possibilities)

Secular occasions:

- *8 Feb* (1828) Jules Verne, science fiction author, born
- *12 Feb* (1709) Alexander Selkirk rescued from the uninhabited island of Juan Fernandez. Daniel Defoe based *Robinson Crusoe* on Selkirk's experiences. (Drama could explore loneliness; self-sufficiency; 'who is my neighbour' etc)
- *4 Mar* (1824) Sir William Hillary founded Royal National Lifeboat Institution
- *5 Mar* (1790) Flora Macdonald died – remembered for her loyalty to Bonnie Prince Charlie, and helping him escape
- *16 Mar* (1912) Captain Oates died on Scott's expedition to the South Pole
- *18 Mar* (1890) John Luther Jones died at the controls of his runaway locomotive, trying to save the lives of his passengers. The story was immortalised in the song 'Casey Jones'.
- *20 Mar* (1857) *Uncle Tom's Cabin* by Harriet Beecher Stowe published. Helped in the campaign to abolish slavery.

April

Religious occasions:

Ascension Day	celebrated with rogation processions and prayers – originally pagan pleas for good crops. Some parishes 'beat the bounds' at this time. In Derbyshire, villagers 'dress' wells with flowers – a custom started by villagers of Tissington in gratitude for surviving the Black Death of 1350

Secular occasions:
- *2 April* (1801) Nelson turned a 'blind eye' at the Battle of Copenhagen
- *3 April* (1860) Pony Express mail service began in the USA
- *10 April* (1829) William Booth born, founder of the Salvation Army
- *15 April* (1912) the *Titanic* sank – once described as 'the unsinkable ship'
- 17 April (1492) Columbus set out on a voyage of exploration which resulted in the European discovery of America. (Good dramatic possibilities linked with courage/going 'into the unknown'.)
- *23 April* – St George's Day. The patron saint of England, St George is famed for killing a legendary dragon. The town associated with the story is Sylene in Libya

May

Religious occasions:

Wesak	great Buddhist festival celebrating the birth, enlightenment and death of the Buddha. Festivities last three days – flowers and lanterns decorate buildings, candles are lit; spectacular processions; presents given to the poor and caged birds set free.
St Augustine's Day	26 May. Canterbury Cathedral now stands on the site of the monastery founded by Augustine, who came to preach in Britain in 597

Secular occasions:
- *8 May* Red Cross Day – the organisation was founded by Henri Dunant after the Battle of Solferino, Italy, in 1859
- *12 May* (1820) Florence Nightingale born (could lead to much dramatic work on nurses, doctors, people who help us . . .)
- *20 May* (1929) Charles Lindberg made solo flight across the Atlantic in *Spirit of St Louis* (good illustration for the theme of courage)

June

Religious occasions:

Shavuoth (Jewish Feast of Weeks)	summer festival celebrating corn harvest – food for mind and body. Special food is eaten, eg *blintzes* (cheese fritters)
St Peter's Day	29 June – good opportunities for dramatic enactment of scenes from his life (Acts of the Apostles)
St Alban's Day	the first British Christian martyr

Secular occasions:
- *2 June* (1953) Queen Elizabeth II crowned
- *4 June* (1940) end of the Dunkirk evacuation, World War II
- *6 June* (1944) 'D-Day' Allied invasion of Normandy – these two dates could be linked in a dramatic consideration of the horror of war
- *27 June* 1880 Helen Keller born – she was blind and deaf, but thanks to a brilliant teacher, Anne Sullivan, she learned to speak. Later wrote *The Story of my Life* and spent the rest of her life fund-raising for schools and homes for blind and deaf children

July

Religious occasions:

St Christopher's Day	legend tells that St Christopher carried a child across a river. The child grew heavier and heavier – and proved to be Christ. St Christopher is patron saint of travellers

Secular occasions:
- *15 July* St Swithin's Day – this is a useful time in the school year to develop a 'mini theme' around the story (see page 130)
- *16 July* (1439) an act banning kissing was passed in an attempt to stop the spread of plague – usesful links with drama considering modern medicine and health care

Bible stories which have dramatic potential

The man who built his house on rock (Matthew 7: 24–27)
Forgiveness: the story of the two debtors (Matthew 18: 23–34)
Actions speak louder than words (Matthew 21: 28–31)
The wise and foolish virgins (Matthew 25: 1–11)
The parable of the talents (Matthew 25: 14–30; Luke 19: 12–24)
Judging others: the splinter in your friends's eye (Luke 6: 41–42)
The good Samaritan (Luke 10: 30–36)
'Knock, and the door will be opened.' (Luke 11: 5–8)
The man who stored up his wealth (Luke 12: 16–20)
The master who returned unexpectedly (Luke 12: 42–46)
Choosing a seat at the wedding (Luke 14: 8–10)
The guests who refused to attend a feast (Luke 14: 16–21)
Forward planning – thinking of the consequences (Luke 14: 28–32)
The lost sheep/coin (Luke 15: 3–10)
The prodigal son (Luke 15: 11–32)
The rich man and Lazarus (Luke 16: 19–31)
The Pharisee and the tax collector (Luke 18: 10–14)

2 Drama development

This section offers suggestions as to how two of the dramatic 'starter' ideas listed in *Drama suggestions* might be developed.

Festival of St Nicholas (6 December)

A The following activity is simple and somewhat static, but it is useful in drawing attention to details of the story. At the start, a child reader says:

Here are some of the things we know about St Nicholas.

As each of the statements below is read out, other children walk across the presenting area carrying objects (or pictures) to represent what is said.

Saint Nicholas was a bishop in the country we now know as Turkey.
Saint Nicholas is the patron saint of children and sailors.
His sign is three golden balls.
He leaves presents in stockings and shoes.
At Amsterdam in Holland he arrives in a ship to give out presents.

B This dramatic activity could be a re-telling of the best-known story about St Nicholas, through a series of readings. With only a little rehearsal it should be possible to synchronise the readings with some mimed action, as follows.
Reading:

Sad things happened in the town where St Nicholas lived. Many people there were very poor. Amongst them was an old man. He had lost all his money and was very sad. He had three daughters – but now he had no money, nobody would marry them. In those days a bride had to take a sum of money with her when she got married. The old man and his daughters were very miserable.

The old man appears and mimes his distress. He points to his daughters as they appear on scene. The daughters also mime unhappiness.

St Nicholas heard about this sad story. He decided to help. He went to a cupboard where he kept his gold and filled a small bag with it. Waiting until it was dark, he crept silently through the streets until he reached the house where the old man lived with his three daughters. Making sure there was nobody about, St Nicholas tiptoed up to an open window and threw the bag of gold in.

St Nicholas goes to the cupboard and fills the bag with gold. Then he walks stealthily through the streets and throws the gold through the window.

Next morning the eldest girl of the house woke up and found a bag of gold lying on her bedroom floor. 'I wonder how that got there?' she thought. Then she took it to her father. He was pleased. 'Now you can get married,' he said. The girl's sisters, however, were very sad. There was no gold for them.

The girl discovers the gold and mimes amazement. She goes to tell her father and sisters; display of mixed emotions – the relief/delight/sadness of the eldest daughter; mixture of disappointment and 'trying not to show it' of the other two girls.

St Nicholas was back in his palace. He knew exactly how the people in the poor man's house would be feeling – but he had plans for that night! As darkness approached he went again to the cupboard of gold. There he took out another small bag and filled it with gold. Once again he crept through the dark streets until he came to the house. Looking carefully about, he saw nobody, and then threw the second bag of gold through the window.

Repeat of the action as above.

The next morning, in the house of the poor man, the second daughter was delighted because she too found a bag of gold. This time, the youngest daughter was not so disappointed. 'If this kind person has sent gold for both of my sisters I am sure he will remember me,' she said to her father. 'I agree, my dear,' replied her father. 'Perhaps he will come again tonight. I think I must make some arrangements in case he does.'

The girls mime excitement over the arrival of second bag of gold; conversation between father and youngest daughter. Father ponders as he makes his plans.

The following night two things happened. St Nicholas went again to the cupboard of gold and filled another small bag. Then, creeping through the darkness again, he headed for the familiar house.

The poor man was determined to find out who was being so kind to his family. So he left his house and hid behind a bush. From this hiding place he could see the front door of his house – and anybody who came near it. As there was a full moon he would be able to recognise any person he saw.

St Nicholas got nearer to the house. Seeing nobody around, again he threw his third bag of gold through the window. As he then turned to go, the poor man stepped out from behind the bush and took St Nicholas by the arm.

'My lord,' said the poor man, 'I thought it might be you who was doing this. There aren't many people who would be so kind and thoughtful.'

'Oh, you gave me a shock,' replied St Nicholas. 'I'm just glad I was able to help. But please, don't tell anybody about this, will you?'

The old man just smiled and said thank you again.

St Nicholas prepares for his third trip; the poor man stealthily takes up his position; throwing the gold; the discovery and the conversation.

Finally, all the actors and readers appear at the front of the presentation area and events are concluded with the following reading:

Good stories tend to spread quickly and soon everybody in town had heard of St Nicholas' kindness to the old man and his three daughters. The story then spread far and wide throughout the world. Today, when we see St Nicholas' sign of the three golden balls, we are reminded of the three bags of gold he gave away to the old man's daughter.

Caring for pets

This second development of a dramatic "starter" idea is built around the old Italian folk tale concerning the Bell of Atri. Here again the drama progesses through readings which relate to appropriate action.

'Nobody in this town need ever worry about getting help,' said the King. 'All they have to do is pull this rope and a bell will ring. Someone will then be sure to help.'

The townspeople are gathered in the town sqaure. The king indicates the rope which rings a bell at the top of a tower.

Because the people of the town of Atri were kind nobody needed to pull the rope for years. The bell got rusty and the rope tattered.

Then one day a pitifully thin horse staggered into the town square. He was so hungry that he started to eat the bell rope. As he pulled the rope – the bell began to ring.

The 'horse' enters the square and after appropriate action, begins to 'eat' the bell rope, resulting in the tolling of the bell. (Off-stage sound effects could be used here.)

When the people of the town heard the bell ringing they dashed out of their houses. They were amazed at what they saw.

Various townspeople dash onto the stage, amazed that the bell has rung, and are equally amazed that it is a horse who is ringing it. Lots of comments such as 'Look at that poor horse . . . he hasn't eaten for weeks' etc

Soon the noise of the bell brought the king to the town square. He took one look at the horse and said to his servants: 'Find out who owns this poor horse and bring him to me.'

Arrival of the king and servants; space made for him; king sends servants off on their mission.

It was found that the horse had once been a favourite pet of an old soldier who lived near the town. Once the horse got too old to ride the soldier did not bother to feed it, and he eventually just turned it out.

Once he heard what had happened in the town square, and he had been brought before the king he was ashamed of his behaviour. He took the horse back and looked after it well until it died years later.

King telling the soldier what the horse had done; soldier asks forgiveness; takes horse home with him after stroking and behaving affectionately to it.

At the end, all the actors and actresses and readers appear at the front of the presenting area and events are concluded by the following reading:

By pulling the rope and ringing the bell the old horse was able to tell all the people of Atri that his owner had not looked after him properly. Most animals and pets cannot 'tell' anybody about their troubles. Let us therefore pray this morning for the RSPCA who help poor and unwanted animals. Let us also pray for all pet owners and hope that they will always look after their animals as well as they possibly can.

3 Scripted plays

This section selects two of the dramatic starter ideas listed in *Dramatic suggestions* and provides a completely scripted play for each.

Actions speak louder than words

This play relates to two of the 'starter' ideas in section 1: 'Actions speak louder than words' – the title, and the story in Matthew 21, 28–31.

The reading of this play could be rehearsed beforehand and then done for an assembly. Alternatively it could be read and taped in the classroom. The tape could then be amplified and played for an assembly whilst the presenters mimed the action. A third possibility is to supplement the reading of the script by an overhead projector showing of pictures related to the action as it develops.

Whichever presentation is used the end product should stimulate a good deal of post-assembly discussion.

Characters

Father; Mother; their two sons – Paul and John; their daughter – Ruth

Time/Location

Long ago in the time when Jesus was alive, on a large farm.

SCENE 1   *At home, supper time*
Father   What are we having for supper?

Mother   We've got some fresh bread, some lovely meat and then a big bunch of juicy grapes.

Paul   Hasn't it been hot today?

John   Too hot.

Father   Too hot or not – we've got a lot of work to do tomorrow.

Ruth   What do you mean 'we' Dad?

Father   Well, John, Paul and I must work in the fields sowing seeds. You will have to bring our dinner to us.

Ruth   Will you start work early?

Mother   They will be up and off as soon as it is light.

Paul   Do we have to? It's too hot to work.

John   Stop complaining Paul. I'll be there on time, Dad.

Father   Good.

Paul   I'm not looking forward to working in that heat.

John   Who cares about the heat?

Father   Well I'm going to bed to get a good sleep.

SCENE 2   *At home, the next morning*

Mother   Drink this before you go out.

Paul   Thanks mother.

Ruth   I'll bring you some bread and cheese, olives and raisins at dinner time.

Father   Where's John?

Ruth   He said he would be up first. I'll go and get him. (*noise of Ruth leaving*)

Father   We can't wait. We've got to get started.

Paul   Hmmmm.

Mother   It will take a long time for three of you to do the work.

Ruth	I've just been to see John. He says he has got a headache. He will follow you to the fields.
Father	I hope he doesn't take long. Come on Paul.
Mother	Goodbye.
Ruth	Bye – see you at dinner time.

SCENE 3   *In the fields, dinner time*

Father	I can see Ruth coming.
Paul	Thank goodness for that.
Father	I wonder where your brother is?
Paul	Not here! We'll be lucky to finish by nightfall if he doesn't hurry up.
Father	Hmm.
Ruth	Hello Dad, hello Paul.
Paul	Hello Sis. What have you got?
Ruth	Bread, water, wine, olives, raisins and some goat's cheese.
Father	Ruth.
Ruth	Yes Dad.
Father	What about John? Why isn't he here?
Ruth	He should be here. He set off ages ago.
Father	Well as you can see, he isn't here.
Paul	Hey, this cheese is great.
Ruth	Good, there's plenty more.
Father	Eat up Paul, we've got a lot to do.
Paul	We'd get it done a lot quicker if John was here.
Ruth	I wonder where he can be?
Father	Come on, back to work.

SCENE 4   *In the fields. It is almost dark*

Father	Nearly finished at last.

Paul   My back is killing me.

Father   There's somebody coming.

Paul   It's mother and Ruth.

Mother   Hello you two, we've brought you some wine and water to drink.

Ruth   And some raisins to eat.

Paul   Sounds good. I think when I stop work I'll fall asleep standing up.

Mother   But . . . where's John?

Father   You tell us!

Ruth   He came home after dinner. He said he had been on his way to the fields when he met a friend.

Mother   The friend asked him to do a favour . . .

Paul   But what about this afternoon?

Mother   I don't know.

Father   It has taken Paul and me hours longer to do this work.

Paul   Because there's only been two of us instead of three.

Father   He promised . . .

Ruth   Look! There's somebody coming . . .

Mother   It's John.

John   (*gasping*) Sorry I'm late. I met Mark and he wanted to show me his new sheep and . . .

Father   You promised.

John   Sorry Dad . . . I'll start early tomorrow. I promise.

Paul   The job is finished.

John   Well . . . I . . .

The king who learned his lesson
The second scripted drama in this section relates to one of the 'anniversary' dramatic possibilities (see page 168). King Canute died on 12 November 1035. The well known story of his chastising of the waves contains the sort of 'moral message' which very young children recognise quickly.

Characters
King Canute; Ladies of the Court: Matilda, Maud, Mary; Knights: Sir Lance, Sir Harold, Sir Gareth; Mark – a small boy; Narrator.

Time/Location
Britain long ago, in the time when Canute was King.

SCENE 1   *The King's palace.*

Narrator	There once lived a brave king called Canute. Although he came from a country called Denmark he became King of all England. A great feast was prepared to celebrate this.
Matilda	Is everything ready for the feast?
Maud	The servants have put out the tables.
Mary	The cook has got all the food ready.
Matilda	The King will be pleased.
Maud	When everyone is here the food will be brought.
Mary	Here comes Sir Lance.
Sir Lance	Good day, ladies – the hall looks magnificent.
Matilda	Thank you sir – and the food will be just as good.
Sir Lance	Ah, here comes Harold.
Sir Harold	Good day Lance, good day ladies.

Ladies	Good day Sir Harold.
Sir Harold	Make sure I am sitting next to the King. I have something important to say to him.
Maud	It will be done, Sir Harold.
Mary	Another knight is coming.
Matilda	It is Sir Gareth.
Maud	Doesn't he look brave?
Sir Gareth	Good day everybody.
Ladies, Harold and Lance	Good day.
Sir Gareth	Bow your heads please- the King is on his way. . . His Majesty, King Canute.
Everybody	Your Majesty.
Canute	Please sit – bring in the food.
Matilda	Servants – the food at once!
Sir Lance	What is this they are bringing . . . goose . . . and duck . . . .
Sir Lance	And look at that wine.
Sir Harold	Ladies and gentlemen. Please stand and drink your wine for England's greatest ever King.
Everybody	The King!
Canute	Thank you, thank you. Now please, let us eat.
Sir Harold	Your Majesty – every bit of England is now yours.
Sir Lance	Not quite every bit.
Sir Harold	What do you mean sir?

Sir Lance	Well – if you go down to the beach, every day the waves wash up and cover it. That bit of England belongs to the sea.
Sir Harold	Pah – if he wanted to, our great King could put a stop to that.
Sir Lance	Oh – how?
Sir Harold	Well . . .er . . .You could stop the waves, couldn't you, your Majesty?
Canute	Hmm? Oh yes . . . yes indeed.
Sir Harold	Tomorrow we will carry the King on his throne down to the beach. Then we'll see who is King over every bit of England!

SCENE 2 *On the seashore*

Narrator	And so the next morning everyone went to the beach. King Canute's men carried him on his throne, and put the throne at the edge of the water . . .
Sir Harold	Your Majesty, no waves would dare to wet your feet.
Sir Lance	The King is right at the edge of the water.
Sir Gareth	And the waves are coming up the beach!
Matilda	I wonder what is going to happen?
Mary	Isn't it exciting!
Maud	Look, the King is going to speak.
Canute	Waves! I command you to come no further. Do not dare to wet my feet!
Sir Lance	The water is still coming in . . .
Sir Gareth	It's getting closer . . .
Matilda	Oh!

Mary	It's come all over the King's feet!
Canute	Waves! Go back – and do not return!
Maud	The waves are going out!
Matilda	They are still going out.
Sir Lance	Now they're turning back.
Sir Gareth	The waves are coming in again.
Matilda	The King is getting his feet wet again!
Maud	. . . and his legs.
Mary	The water is splashing all round him.
Sir Lance	That boy – what is he doing?
Sir Gareth	He is running down the beach to say something to the King.
Mark	Sir – Sir – you must not stay here. The waves come in very quickly and you will be drowned.
Canute	Do you know who I am, boy?
Mark	No sir, but it doesn't matter. These waves will drown anybody.
Canute	Come with me lad . . .
	(*Canute and Mark move to where knights and ladies are gathered*)
Canute	Now, Sir Harold – you see the foolishness of what you say. This lad here is right – no man, whether he is King or not, can turn back the waves. That is God's work.

Appendix 1: Music

Music plays an important part in infant and first school assemblies, and most schools have a repertoire of records, tapes and music books to cater for this need. These generally reflect the personal or collective tastes of the staff, and the recommendations made here are, similarly, a personal choice. In making this selection, I have borne the following considerations in mind:

1   All the material has been used extensively with young children;
2   The music books recommended mostly contain items which can be played by any reasonably competent pianist;
3   The recorded material is of two kinds:
    a   music to establish a variety of 'moods' in assemblies;
    b   recordings of children's singing, of a high quality. This can be used either to set a standard, or for 'singalong' purposes.

Music books

Every complete assembly in the first section of this book includes a hymn suggestion. All these are taken from the excellent BBC publication *Come and Praise*. It may be, however, that something different is occasionally required for a class or choir performance; for a special occasion; or to give variety. When this is the case, the following anthologies should prove useful.

Every colour under the sun selected by Barbara Cass-Beggs, Redvers Brandling and others. Ward-Lock Educational, 1983.
These 'songs on thoughtful themes for primary school assemblies' – 55 in all – were chosen to relate to the following themes: the seasons; the world around us; identity; prayer; work and everyday life; helping others and social awareness; working for a better world; co-operation and tolerance; celebrations; beginnings and endings.

A musical calendar of festivals selected by Barbara Cass-Beggs. Ward-Lock Educational, 1983.
This lovely book has groupings of songs listed month-by-month from January to December. As well as music and words, most items also have useful pieces of additional information.

Tinder box selected by Sylvia Barrat and Sheena Hodge. A and C Black, 1982.
A collection of 66 songs for young children, particularly valuable for assemblies in that they relate to children's experiences: their fears; quarrels; laughter and celebrations; and relationships with friends and family.

Sing a song of celebration Mary Martin and Valerie Stumbles. Holt, Rinehart and Winston, 1984.
The authors of this book are well known as producers of splendid music and words for infant children. This is a valuable volume for use in assembly, with music and words related to: Harvest; Halloween; 5 November; Christmas; New Year; Pancake Day; Mother's Day; Easter; Spring; May Day; birthdays; outings; sports day and holidays.

The burning bush music by Jim Parker, words by Tom Stanier. Chappell Music Ltd, 1980.
These songs about the story of Moses were originally written for a BBC Schools Television series, *Watch*, and a recorded version is also available (*Watch again*, REC 375). Each song is delightful in its own right.

Recorded Music

Music to set a mood
Young children respond readily to 'mood' and a good way to establish this is through recorded music. The following list of records offers a wide range of possibilities.

Scheherazade (EMI CFP 174) This is superb preparatory music for story telling, in particular the track 'The young prince and the young princess'.
The André Previn music festival (EMI ESDW 720) This two-record set has a very good range of material, including 'Greensleeves'; 'The Sorcerer's Apprentice; 'The Emperor Waltz' etc.
Negro spirituals anthology No 2 by the Golden Gate Quartet (Columbia/EMI 2C 062 11993) Gospel singing, with its jazz elements, is often effective in assembly. This record is worth getting for one track alone, the superb 'Take my hand precious Lord'.
Sound – wide screen (Decca MOR 9) This is 'big' music, including many familiar themes, such as those from 'Fiddler on the roof', 'The third man' etc.

Echoes of Italy (Decca PFS 4174) For assemblies requiring a 'warm' or holiday theme this is a useful record, with tracks such as 'Quando, quando, quando' and 'Al di la'.

The world of military bands (Decca SPA 18) 'Rousing' is the best description here with lively renderings of 'Colonel Bogey,' 'Lili Marlene' etc.

Space invaders – BBC themes (BBC REH 442) This is a useful record for creating atmosphere, containing themes from programmes such as 'Star Trek,' 'Dr Who' etc.

Singalong Music

Come and Praise (BBC REC 317) An invaluable addition to any school record collection, the high standard of singing on this record can be used to encourage and stimulate the quality of children's music making.

The Church of England Children's Society, Old Town Hall, Kennington Road, London SE11 4QD is another good source for 'singing' records for use with young children in assembly. Three 45rpms which can be thoroughly recommended are:

There's room in our house Contents: 'Somebody needs you'; 'Find another way'; 'There's room in our house'; 'Waifs and strays'; 'Splash!'

Everybody's children Contents: 'Everybody's children'; 'Watch them grow'; 'The sunflower';

An old fashioned Christmas Contents: 'An old fashioned Christmas'; 'Here's a health'; 'Little match girl'; 'Put a candle in the window'.

Appendix 2: Sources

I am a firm believer in material being assimilated and then re-told in infant and first school assemblies. With this principle in mind, sources of suitable material are as varied as they are many.

Contemporary material

1 Newspapers offer a regular supply of stories about courage, fortitude etc. A file of cuttings is a valuable addition to any assembly presenter's armoury. Local newspapers are often particularly useful.

2 The 'Letters page' in many women's magazines is also a useful source of interesting and rewarding stories.

3 Magazines linked to organisations can provide interesting items. A good example is *Satellite*, the magazine for Young Save the Children (can be contacted at Grove Lane, London SE5 8RD).

4 Stories about animals provide valuable assembly material. The following organisations offer useful information:

Hearing Dogs for the Deaf 105 Gower Street, London WC1E 6AH. (Information on the Royal National Institute for the Deaf and it training scheme regarding dogs and deaf people.)

Guide Dogs for the Blind Alexandra House, 9–11 Park Street, Windsor, Berks SL4 1JR.

PRO Dogs The Dog House, 4 New Road, Ditton, Maidstone, Kent. (Details of a beneficial scheme by which old and sick people have regular contact with companion animals.)

Society for Companion Animal Studies New Malden House, 1 Blagdon Road, New Malden, Surrey KT3 4TB

(A study group which examines the bond between people and animals.)

Joint Advisory Committee on Pets in Society Walter House, 418–422 Strand, London WC2R 0PL.
PDSA South Street, Dorking, Surrey RH4 2LB
(Various materials, including a pamphlet on caring for injured and young birds.)
5   News programmes on TV and radio also yield stories which can be adapted for infant assemblies.

Religious material

Clearly this has to come from a variety of cultures. Almost all the sources available need to be assimilated and then re-told.

For a simple re-telling of Christian stories there is still no better book than *New World– the best of the New Testament in plain English* Alan T Dale, Oxford University Press 1967. A useful set of books from which assembly material can be taken is *The Lion Story Bible* (Lion Publishing). This series contains 30 Old Testament books and 21 New Testament books; all are written for children and well illustrated.

For material connected to other religions there are some excellent assembly compendiums, containing a wide variety of stories which can be adapted. Particularly recommended are:
The assembly year Robert Fisher, Collins Educational 1985.
Assembly stories from around the world   William Dargue, Oxford University Press 1983.

Another valuable source of varied religious (and other) material is the magazine *Hands together*, published twice a term by Scholastic Publications, Marlborough House, Holly Walk, Leamington Spa, Warks CV32 4LS.

Finally in this category there is an excellent series called *Celebrations* (Ginn) which includes small individual books on Diwali, Hanukka and Eid-ul-Fitr.

Folk tales

There are many collections of folk tales which yield useful assembly material. Sometimes small parts of a story can be used to illustrate specific points. The following are especially helpful:
Tales from the Panchatantra retold by Leonard Clark, Evans 1979.
The illustrated book of world fables Yong Yap Cotterell, Windward 1979. (Material from this book must always be read and 'vetted' in advance, because it contains some stories which are very crude – both in conception and in language.)

My first big story book Richard Bamberger, Puffin 1969.
Folk tales of India (a 21-volume collection) and *Folk tales of the world* (11 books) Sterling Publishers.
The Ramayana retold by Elizabeth Seeger, Dent 1975.
Egyptian and Sudanese folk tales retold by Helen Mitchnik, Oxford University Press 1978.
Armenian folk tales and fables Charles Downing, Oxford University Press 1972. (This book offers an enormous selection of Armenian proverbs. Many of these provide excellent 'thoughts' for assembly, eg
'You cannot draw a straight line with a crooked ruler.'
'One has to knock on seven doors for one to open.'
'Temptation does not announce its coming.')
Listen to this story Grace Hallworth, Methuen 1977.
Fables from Aesop retold by James Reeves, Blackie 1977.
Tales from the South Pacific Islands told by Anne Gittins, Stemmer House 1977. (This book is an absolute gem! It consists of stories collected by Mrs Gittins when she was the wife of a colonial administrator, and can be read with satisfaction and delight at any level.)
Tokoloshi African folk tales retold by Diana Pitcher, Skilton and Shaw 1980.
A world of folk tales James Riordan, Hamlyn 1981. (This beautifully-produced book contains much useful material.)
Folk tales from Asia for children everywhere sponsored by the Asian Cultural Centre for UNESCO, Weatherhill/Heibonsha 1975.
The lion on the path and other African stories retold by Hugh Tracey, Routledge and Kegan Paul 1967.
Italian folk tales Italo Calvino, Dent 1975.